Praise for Acous

Want to rock your leadership role, and deal with others in a way that inspires results? Rick Lozano's message resonates, offering both realistic and creative ways to amplify your impact without driving others away. No matter what you are negotiating at work, if you are leading a project, a team, a department, or an organization-read this book!

—Linda Swindling, JD, CSP, Best-selling author of more than 20 books including *Ask Outrageously! The Secret to Getting What You Really Want and Stop Complainers and Energy Drainers: How to Negotiate Work Drama to Get More Done*

Rick offers a refreshing perspective on leadership that inspired new ways of thinking and interacting in practical ways.

—Merit Kahn, CEO, SELLect Sales

You know the tune that you keep singing in your head? That's how Acoustic Leadership is spinning in my head; on a loop because I connected with it and can remember its essence. Reading Acoustic Leadership is like having a conversation with the author Rick Lozano versus another dry business book. It stirs up emotions, reflection, and aha's that are easy to implement. The book builds like a concert; at the start you can hear the roar of the crowd, you can picture the scene, and then Rick strikes a chord and your whole view of leadership changed. If you're ready to join the concert and learn how to soar in your leadership journey, then grab your copy and get ready for an acoustic ride.

—Laura Bonich, CEO, The Leaders' Lighthouse

Acoustic Leadership was the leadership book I didn't know I needed to read. Rick mentions in the book that there are nearly 560 million other ideas on being a better leader. There's no doubt that this should be at the very top of that list. Thanks for helping me turn into a better leader, Rick!

—Taylorr Payne, CEO, SpeakerFlow

Rick integrates the same energy musicians use to connect with their audiences with insightful research and years of experience developing leaders who inspire – and the output? A leadership book that rocks!

—Britt Andreatta, Ph.D., Best-selling author of the Wired To series

It's easy to see "another leadership book" and groan - which is exactly why Acoustic Leadership is such a breath of fresh air. Using tried-and-true leadership methods as the backbone, Rick is able to capture the theory behind the methods in a refreshingly new and compelling way. Acoustic Leadership combines great storytelling with relevant insight and practical solutions. Not only is it helpful in creating a leadership culture that resonates, it is fun to read!

—Austin Grammon, President, SpeakerFlow

Music has an incredible power to move us and Rick Lozano's application to leadership is unique and refreshing. This book is full of lightbulb moments and actionable takeaways. Similar to that moment in a pub when everyone is heartily engaged in a rousing sing-along, Acoustic Leadership is an emotional connection and an invitation for us to all participate as leaders.

—Irvine Nugent, Ph.D., Author – Leadership Lessons from the Pub

ACOUSTIC
LEADERSHIP

Develop a Leadership
Culture That Resonates

RICK LOZANO

UNLOCK&
AMPLIFY®

Unlock & Amplify Media
San Antonio, Texas

Acoustic Leadership: Develop A Leadership Culture That Resonates
© Copyright 2021 by Rick Lozano

Unlock & Amplify Media
San Antonio, Texas

This edition May 2021.

Acoustic Leadership® and Unlock & Amplify® are registered trademarks of Rick Lozano. All rights reserved, use by written permission only.

Amplified Ideas™, and The Muck and the Magic™, are trademarks of Rick Lozano, pending registration with the USPTO at time of print. All rights reserved.

Edited by Jenefer Angell at Passionfruit Projects

Additional editing and proofreading by Regina Pfohl

Front and back cover, artwork and design by Erica Russell at ELR Design

Book layout and additional design by Tim Slade.

For speaking engagements, leadership development or consulting inquiries, orders or bulk purchases of this book, please email rickl@ricklozano.com.

ISBN: 978-1-7348353-0-4 (paper)

ISBN: 978-1-7348353-1-1 (eBook)

For Angela.

Contents

Contents

III. The Wrap-Up

The Why

Sky's the limit so you know I'm gonna rise and shine
I gotta do my thing,
I'm kinda getting a little tired of all that's hidden
That's the reason I'ma speak my mind, keep from goin insane

—C. Douglas, L. Hubbard, S. Storch,
A. Thompson, W. Thompson,
T. Trotter, and C. Walker

Five hundred sixty-one million.
Yes, million.

I know, big number. Want to guess what it represents? The number of songs written since The Beatles arrived on the scene? Perhaps. The number of grains of sand in a school playground? Maybe. Number of stars in a neighboring galaxy? Could be.

But in this case, we're talking about five hundred sixty-one million suggestions. Hits. Ideas that appeared four years ago when I first began this project and entered the phrase "how to be a better leader" into a Google search. In less than three-quarters of a second, the world's mightiest search engine served up over half a billion recommendations, each just a click away. Instant access to the planet's collective knowledge, all the answers a person could ever possibly need to become a better leader. What more could I ask?

And it is all on the internet, so you know it is all true. ;)

(Question…have we reached a point yet where it is acceptable for an author to use emojis in a book? Oh well, I don't care! My book, my emoji!)

Where was I? Oh, yes. Five hundred sixty-one million ideas for being a better leader. This begs the question…

Do we *need* another leadership book?
Or, rather, why are you reading another leadership book? Maybe that's a better question.

Are you hoping to develop further as a leader? Do you notice a lack of effective leadership in your organization? Could you use some help getting your leaders aligned on a common approach? Are you frustrated with your leaders? All great questions, and the clearer we get on our WHY, the clearer we will be on the HOW. This book will help with both of those.

Or if you're just the type of person who reads every leadership book that comes out, cool!
Welcome!

In any case, my answer to the question, "Do we need another leadership book?" is pretty clear: Yes.

Two reasons:

1. *We are still figuring it out.* Despite all the best ideas, the most insightful literature, the biggest and brightest minds telling us how leadership should work, we still struggle. We can turn to the Simon Sineks of the world who shine a light on the truth; we can access the opinions of millions of authors via the interwebs. And even with all of this, workplace engagement still can be wildly difficult to navigate. And yes, leaders still have a huge role to play in that dynamic. And,

2. *Information without emotion means nothing.* All the world's best ideas are essentially meaningless if you look at the words and don't elicit an emotional response significant enough to drive action. I wrote *Acoustic Leadership: Develop a Leadership Culture That Resonates* to add some passion to the conversation. Leaders deserve it. So many are already out there doing fantastic work — but many others could more effectively reach their leadership potential with a few adjustments to help them reimagine and reprioritize their actions. Still more leaders don't even know they are leaders yet, and connecting emotionally to this information might also connect them to their voice and purpose.

And the world is full of people desperate for authentic leadership.

So here we are. Welcome to the five hundred sixty-one million and first idea on leadership development! 😊

Who is this book for?

You, obviously!

This book is for emerging leaders and the people who lead and develop them. It is for people who support, coach, work with, and foster (hopefully) better leaders in their organizations. It's for those of you who are leaders and don't yet know it. It is for long-time leaders looking for a bit of inspiration or guidance on how to do even better. This book is for CEOs and senior leaders who are, rightfully, concerned about their company cultures and succession planning. This book is for human resource professionals, learning and talent development professionals, and consultants. This book is for you.

I hope *Acoustic Leadership*® offers a refreshing point of view and a different perspective. A fresh take on a familiar tune.

I'm glad you are here. Let's create something great together.

What are you going to learn?

In Part I, we introduce the problem and discuss the numerous opportunities facing us as organizations, leaders, and developers of leaders. We will explore the benefits of a change in our approach with highlighted examples of behaviors and traditions we've become accustomed to that aren't serving us well.

Then, as promised, Part II introduces three foundations to help develop a resonant leadership culture that builds great leaders and amplifies organizational power:

- *Simplicity:* Let's make it simple for people to do their best work. It pays off.
- *Authenticity:* Leadership is all about relationships, so let's develop authentic and safe ones built on trust and accountability.
- *Opportunity:* It's the greatest gift a leader can give. Let's explore ways to offer even better opportunities — for leaders and the people they lead — and expand our leadership perspectives beyond the traditional definitions and confines.

Additionally, we'll explore examples of companies and leaders across the globe who are succeeding where others struggle, and you will be able to identify opportunities and areas that you can focus on or tweak to become a more effective leader and engender a culture that produces resonant leaders in your organizations, your teams, and your world.

In Part III, I challenge you to convert inspiration into action and commit to changes that create the resonant leadership culture you can build. I end with gratitude and the story of how this all came into being and the leader whose impact made it possible.

Along the way, I've included several call-out sections called Amplified Ideas™, that give you action items to implement that will assist you in making meaningful changes in your daily routine.

The Acoustic Leadership framework does not intend to answer every existing leadership challenge. No one model can do that, and anyone who claims that they have the be-all and end-all solution is trying to sell you something. Like their book. 😊

Wait. Well, okay, I have sold you a book, and it does offer solutions. But I hope that you, like me, don't believe in absolutes or one "right" way to do anything. Everything is subjective, and different scenarios require different approaches, depending on the people involved, the nature of the world, and business. (You get my point.) However, there *are* more and less effective ways of leading people, and we will explore them.

As we go along this journey together, please remember that this book is an invitation to a dialogue about where we are, what we are experiencing, and what we can do to refine our leadership systems in a meaningful and lasting way.

In keeping with the desire for a conversational feel, which is obviously harder to do in a book than in a workshop or presentation, I use the same language I would if you and I were sitting down over a cup of coffee or a cocktail. (You'll notice a few times when we move from a latte to whiskey shots pretty quickly!) And in the spirit of the book's overarching theme of resonance, I apply a musical overlay throughout to add music's natural properties of inspiration and connection to the reading experience.

As The Cat Empire, one of my favorite Australian bands, sings in their song "How to Explain," "music is the language of us all." And I believe it. (I encourage you to check them out and any other musical references included in the book. They've added joy and meaning to my life, and who knows? They might do the same for you. And feel free to send your favorites to the email on the copyright page. I'll include them in a playlist online where we all can discover, perhaps, our new favorite songs.)

I include relevant song lyrics throughout the book to help further connect the information to emotion. I comment on particular versions in the text, referencing the artist that best illustrates my point (or that I like the best), but I attribute each quote to the original songwriters in the chapter openings. I try to think about those foundational details—noticing when the composer is different from the recording artist, or the artist's public name is different from their legal name. They are great reminders of this:

> Songs are *creations* dreamed up by individuals,
> each a unique voice born of an inspired idea.

When done well, at the right intersection of time and space, they become an integral part of society's fabric.

So look for the breadcrumbs, keep an eye out for those details, and if you catch sight of Lady Gaga's real name, remember personas like hers are constructs that take time and effort to develop. The most successful find a path from humble beginnings to a leadership role in the world while remaining true to their original vibe. You have an opportunity to develop or refine your authentic leadership voice right now.

To help crank up your next jam, I end every section with a playlist of my current favorite versions of some of the music referenced in each segment. When you read the lyrics, try to guess the public names of the less apparent songwriters. I've included more details, including the publishing label and year, to help you locate specific versions if you like.

To recap: information without emotion means nothing. And music abounds with emotion. And much like your emotional connections to music morph as you evolve, so does this discussion. Since available evidence is tied to the moment of publication, and knowing how fast the world is changing, do expect to continue asking questions and reevaluate what you know as new revelations arise.

For additional tools, resources, and access to the entire Acoustic Leadership playlist in one place, visit ricklozano.com/resources. I'll continue to add content to help this expedition jump beyond the pages of this book. Oh, and if you really want to hear the true essence of this work, check out the audiobook. It is going to rock!

Okay. Anything else? Ready to get started? Great. Let's roll!

 **Playlist**

Title	Artist	Time
Why (What's Going On)	The Roots; written by C. Douglas, L. Hubbard, S. Storch, A. Thompson, W. Thompson, T. Trotter, C. Walker (Geffen, 2004).	4:20
How To Explain	The Cat Empire; written by H. Hull-Brown, J. Khadiwhala, O. McGill, R. Monro, F. Riebl (Virgin, 2003).	3:38

Visit ricklozano.com/resources for the complete Acoustic Leadership playlist.

I. The Problem

Well, I'm stuck in the middle with you
And I don't know what it is I should do

—G. Rafferty and J. Egan

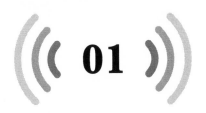

The Magic

> *If I never have a cent*
> *I'd be as rich as Rockefeller*
> *Gold dust at my feet*
> *On the side of the street that's sunny*

—J. McHugh and D. Fields

As the audience fills the theater, they hear a familiar jazz standard played by two musicians lower stage right. They don't know the tune, per se, yet it coerces them to hum along instinctively. They see a tall upright bass player jamming alongside a pianist, shoulders hunched over the keys, lockstep with the groove, fingers traveling from the high to the low registers, and back again.

A man in the fifth row leans to his right to ask his companion a question and begins nodding, his quizzical expression changing to a mixture of surprised enlightenment. The bass player is, indeed, whom he thought: Penn Jillette. One-half of the world-famous act he's here to see, the incredible magic duo of Penn and Teller, live at the appropriately named Penn and Teller Theater at the Rio Hotel in Las Vegas.

Penn Jillette is in the opening act for his own show. Crazy!

Most people filling the seats don't seem to notice. They sit, perusing the show program and finishing their drinks (it is Vegas, after all), talking to their friends while Penn (whom, let's not forget, they are here to see) scans the audience while swinging to the tune. Funny, if you think about it, it's almost as if — to Penn — *they* are the opening act *he's* watching before the show.

The music ends, earning a round of applause from about half of the audience. The duo exits stage left, and the audience gets ready to see the genius that is Penn and Teller, many not knowing that they've already begun.

Okay, wait. Time out. Why are we talking about magicians? Isn't this book supposed to be about leadership?

It is. Slow your roll. I'm building up to something here!

Penn and Teller are not only masters at what they do; they are unique in the way they do it. They astound the audience with the wizardry of some of their "tricks"…and then immediately show them exactly how it is done. They give away their secrets, with step-by-step explanations! Yet, even with the "behind the scenes" intel on how the "magic" works, the audience is still amazed. Night after night for over twenty years running at the Rio.

In one of their famous bits, Teller walks onto the stage. A film noir vibe fills the air. He takes a puff off a cigarette, crushes it out on the floor, then lights a fresh one while Penn plays the upright bass. But as Penn narrates the action, the fans begin to realize that there is, in fact, only one cigarette. They had just witnessed a sleight-of-hand virtuoso at the top of his game. Penn, still vamping on the bass, walks them through the seven fundamental principles of magic in real-time as Teller faces the opposite direction and demonstrates the ruse: palm, ditch, steal, load, simulation, misdirection, and switch. Repeat. (Look it up online. It is awesome. Or better yet, if you have the chance, see them live — they are worth it!)

The show moves on. Penn and Teller display a brilliant combination of art and illusion and, perhaps most amazingly, even though the crowd knows that those seven principles of magic are in play, they continue to ask, "How in the world did they do *that?*" after each new trick.

And even when all of the instructions are plainly laid out, when the exact knowledge of the process is in hand, most people will never be able to replicate the technique and precision mastered by Penn and Teller. They lack the required focus, talent, dedication, accuracy, and execution.

This isn't "magic," per se. This is craftsmanship. And, as Penn and Teller deftly convey with their craft, there are no secrets.

Which brings us to leadership.

We've heard this song before.

Five hundred sixty-one million.

Again, the number of suggestions that appeared when I searched the term "how to be a better leader." In a third of a second. Five hundred sixty-one million ideas on how to be a better leader.

Folks, just as we learned from Penn and Teller, there are no secrets. There's nothing new left to learn here. Not that everything on the internet is true and accurate (understatement), but it has all been said and done. Between the John Maxwells and Jim Collinses of the world, the countless books, the TED Talks, the billions of dollars people and organizations spend on leadership development and summits, the simple truth is...there. Everything is out there!

Don't believe me? Google it!

"So...okay, Rick. Then why am I reading this book?"

Because, my friend, apparently, we *still need it*. Even with five hundred sixty-one million or more ideas, concepts, frameworks, and models for how to be a better leader, the world is always in need of just that. Better leaders.

"Survey Says!"

...that we still have much work to do! Check out these stats. According to Indeed.com, 71 percent of us are currently looking for a new job or are at least open to one should something appear that sounds attractive. And more than half of us — 55 percent — have actively conducted a job search in the last two years. Since the onset of the pandemic, with the rapid "trial-by-fire" immersion into widespread dispersed and work-from-home setups, new challenges have arisen that make the work environment more complicated than ever (for those folks who were able to retain their jobs, that is). And even those fortunate to still be employed are facing burnout on a massive scale and pondering their options.

One year into the COVID-19 era, new data is emerging illustrating the enormity of the challenge. A recent survey done by Microsoft found that 41 percent of the thirty thousand people surveyed globally were ready to pack it up, part ways, and say "peace out!" with the people providing the paychecks. (Ah, the sweet allure of alliteration!)

Why? Why are we so willing to leave? Well, according to Gallup (and the 51 percent of us who said so), it's because we are "just satisfied" with our jobs. Being "just satisfied" makes us vulnerable to suggestion, open to exploring the proverbial "greener grass" somewhere else. And that's not even the most alarming news.

The bad news: 16.5 percent of us are actively disengaged in our jobs, according, again, to Gallup. I probably don't need to tell you, but that sucks! That isn't beneficial for the business, the customers, the employees themselves.

And don't think for a second that employee disengagement doesn't somehow transfer to the customer experience. Of course, it does. It affects both employee and management's willingness to go the extra mile and spend time solving problems; it affects how engaged an employee is willing to be when speaking to customers directly.

And disengagement is a total drag. We spend a large portion of our lives at work. Not wanting to be there only heightens the agony.

And then there's the bottom line. The toll on corporate revenue due to disengaged employees is in the billions of dollars. BILLIONS. (With a BILL! And an IONS.)

Oh, but wait, there is some good news as well, and we need more of that in our lives: the number of people who are engaged currently sits at 34 percent. That may not sound like something worth celebrating, but after years of minor to no improvement, that number represents its highest point since Gallup began reporting it in 2000. So not everything is doom and gloom, my friends!

And to be fair, sometimes leaving a job is an excellent thing for everyone involved. We've all left jobs before because new opportunities came along.

And employee expectations have shifted; if another employer can offer a better work experience, there may be ample reason to switch jobs. Attrition isn't always a sign of bad things happening in the workforce, but we need to understand why it is happening.

But let's also not make excuses. When it comes down to it, amongst all the different reasons people leave, one persistent theme consistently rears its ugly head.

Weak leadership.

"It's not you. It's me."

No, dear leader, it is you.

According to the same Gallup information, managers and leaders account for up to a 70 percent variance in employee engagement. That's a pretty big deal. Anecdotally, people have plenty to say about those in charge, but sticking strictly with the data from the previously referenced Microsoft survey, leaders are also slightly out of touch and having a wildly different work experience compared to their reports. When asked to rate whether they felt they were "thriving" at work, or "surviving/struggling" instead, those with traditional titles and authority identified as "thriving" 61 percent of the time— 23 percentage points higher than those they lead.

> A leader should not be surfing while everyone else struggles to stay afloat.

We have work to do.

Let's Unlock & Amplify® our leadership potential.
But wait, leader friends. I'm here for you. I've got your back.

Our exploration isn't about finding fault. You are not to blame here. (Well, a couple of you are — you know who you are. Actually, no, you probably don't. Look up the Dunning-Kruger effect.) Most of the leaders I know want to be great at their job; they want to be inspiring leaders who make a difference in their teams, business, and the world.

But the world has changed. Fast.

And the COVID-19 situation only accelerated that evolution. Even prior to the pandemic, though, consider the enormous transformation caused by significant advances in the global work environment, particularly in the last decade:

- The rise of virtual, dispersed teams.
- The globalization of supply chains, companies, and workforces.
- New technologies that connect people, information, leaders, and real-time customer service around the world.
- The impact of social media and customer ability to leverage those tools as a means of assistance, complaint, or praise.

All of these factors have transformed the nature of work and our place in it. While streamlining communication and workflow, these transformations have added as much stress as they were supposed to relieve, created more questions around what "efficient" really means, and forced us to evaluate or negotiate our commitments to and with each other. We live in a society of uber plugged-in, multitasking, always "on" workers and leaders. And we are struggling to figure out how to balance it all and maintain our sanity and personal lives in the process.

The teams and leaders I've worked with are well aware of these struggles and are working through different permutations of these challenges as you read this. Leaders in London are making crucial decisions before half their team wakes up in Phoenix. A nervous team member, wondering why no one has responded to their text in the 10 minutes since they sent it. The team that just found out their office is relocating to a different part of the world. The business that no longer shares an office. The new leader who isn't exactly sure how often to check in on their new work-from-home direct report, "I mean, I *trust* them…but how do I know they are *working?*"

Are you picking up what I'm putting down?

Life is different, leaders are swirling in the winds of change, and both employees and leadership are still catching up and dealing with some learning curves.

But, again, let's not make excuses, or rather, let's spread them a little more democratically.

As the world has changed, many of your business haven't.

The novel coronavirus only exacerbated what was already occurring.

As the needs of organizations have evolved, many of the schools of thought regarding leadership haven't. And many leaders, even with new generations filling their talent pool, haven't changed.

And finally — here we go, I'm on a roll here — those of us whose job it is to coach, develop, and support leaders in the process *didn't make it easy!*

There. I said it. (I might lose some friends here. #worthit)

"Does it really have to be this complicated?"

That was the question I kept asking myself.

The year was 2017, and we had been working on this project for weeks, formalizing our company's leadership model to include a comprehensive list of all the leadership competencies our leaders needed to understand and exhibit. (We started calling them "vitals" because everyone hated the term "competencies" by now — that alone should have told us something.)

The intent of crafting our own version of these competency models was to account for (what we considered) our unique culture. To provide clarity, to give insight into what "effective leadership" was here and where there were opportunities to develop. And also, to have a rubric in place to rate how well leaders are doing. (Whatever you do, don't do a search on the internet for leadership rubrics – your brain will not be happy with you.)

Ratings — you know, the thing that impacts how much you get paid and whether you get promoted. Kind of important, don't you think?

Okay, take a deep breath and try to follow me here. Part of our challenge was to map each competency across every level of leadership to illustrate, for example, what creating accountability looked like if you were a vice president and how that looked different if you were a frontline manager, a director, etcetera. Then (as if that wasn't enough,) we were charged with creating three proficiency ranges at each level with definitions for performances that were rated at "above," "below," or "at" the expected level.

If this sounds confusing, that's because it is confusing.

And I wasn't alone in my confusion. The more research I did, the more I found that companies worldwide were engaged in this arduous process to varying degrees. But that gave me no solace. I found myself overwhelmed. I was delicately trying to outline the difference in behavioral expectations between a level 2 and a level 3 proficiency for a particular competency: what does it look like to "cope effectively with ambiguity and vagueness" at level 2 compared to level 3?

I have no idea.

Here's another doozy: how do we measure whether someone "uses logical methods to solve difficult problems with effective solutions"?

Indeed! How do we measure that? And what if, just what if, someone uses completely *illogical methods* to solve problems and it *works*? What then?

"I'm sick of this crap!" I yelled to myself, "Does it have to be this hard?"

The answer is: no, it does not. And I'll offer proof in the coming pages.

Optimization, standardization, and competency-based leadership development approaches also haven't helped our cause. (I'm probably going to lose some (more) friends here.) One of the biggest trends in the last 30 years was the rise of the process-improvement approach to all things business as companies everywhere tried to drive profits and shareholder value, minimize attrition, and ensure quality.

The lean, Six Sigma–type methodologies and organizational tools that used to be production-focused bled into the realm of leadership development. Utilizing a standardized process — valuable for making widgets — as a leadership development tool ended up applying that same "nuts and bolts" approach to people.

And, you might not be surprised to hear, people didn't respond well.

What did we expect?

The levels and ratings model further complicated matters and created confusion during coaching sessions from Dallas to New Delhi. The endless array of assessment tools, which, while valuable as a vehicle for insight and awareness, didn't provide our leadership teams with tools to help deliver specific feedback mechanisms and foster honest and open conversation with their employees.

The context was not provided, for example, when annual performance reviews stated that the person scored a three out of five on "negotiating a win-win situation," even though they had won significant deals in the last quarter and were up for a promotion. What were they supposed to do with that? Why not a five?

And don't hate me for asking the question, but wasn't this whole exercise supposed to provide *clarity*?

Now, to be fair, the competencies and systems we created weren't all that bad compared to some others. Take a peek online at the US Office of Personnel Management Competencies. You'll find six general categories, subdivided into 29 different leadership competencies, mapped across five different leadership levels for a total of <does math in head...resorts to calculator> 145 different shades of dexterity! Really?

True story, yo.

And, come on, how in the world are employees set up for success during the performance review season when the wording that determines their rating includes arbitrary characteristics like the ability to "apply this competency in *exceptionally* difficult situations" versus "apply this competency in *considerably* difficult situations"?

Are you f#@%ing serious?

(I told you I was going to speak as if we were having coffee or cocktails in the intro. That was cocktails.)

Which brings us to the next question.

What do we need from our leaders?

And how do we make it easy for them to succeed?

First and foremost, I believe in creating clarity around leadership expectations with specific behavioral examples. I'm also a fan of transparency around overall employee expectations, for that matter. But I don't think we are setting up leaders *or* employees for success — from a development and performance perspective — when we adhere to cookie-cutter competency templates with vague gradients of behaviors that leave everything up to situational interpretation. They don't tell us who truly is and isn't an "effective leader" nor how anyone is supposed to become one. And here's a question:

What does "effective" leadership look like now?

How has that definition evolved after all the disruptions we've been through globally?

For the sake of alignment, let's get away from any leadership philosophy for the time being and consider this: our businesses, our organizations, our teams, need leaders to — at a very high level — **drive results and engagement**. Great leaders in your organization — you — are responsible for just that. When you scale everything back, temporarily putting aside competencies, frameworks, and models, effective leadership is a balance of driving results and fostering engagement.

And our conversation on leadership isn't just relegated to business. It is essential in life.

We need leaders to inspire us, guide us, equip us with skills and beliefs to bring to life the changes we imagine and need.

So how do we do it? How do we uncomplicate this puzzle? How do we reinterpret a familiar tune so that leadership harmonies result?

Like at Penn and Teller's show, the answers are right in front of us: focus, practice, and execution. I propose three areas of focus as the foundation for Acoustic Leadership that directly impact the desired balance of results and engagement:

- *Simplicity*: Let's make it simple for people to do their best work.
- *Authenticity*: Leadership is all about relationships. Let's build authentic, safe ones based on trust and accountability.
- *Opportunity*: The greatest gift a leader can give is the gift of opportunity. Let's reimagine where those opportunities lie and how we develop people to take advantage of them.

These three areas, combined with a fresh focus, modified approaches, and an upgraded mindset can positively influence leaders and those they lead. In the following pages, I put forth a call to action to make the complex simple, reexamine the nature of leadership, and reframe our understanding of the leader's role for the benefit of the leaders themselves and the people they lead.

Let's do this.

▶ Playlist

Title	Artist	Time
Stuck In The Middle With You	Stealers Wheel; written by G. Rafferty and J. Egan (A&M, 1973).	3:24
On The Sunny Side Of The Street	Nat King Cole; written by J. McHugh and D. Fields (Blue Note Records, digital remaster, 1993).	2:56
On The Sunny Side Of The Street	Penn Jillette and Mike Jones; written by J. McHugh and D. Fields (Capri Records, 2018).	6:11

Visit ricklozano.com/resources for the complete Acoustic Leadership playlist.

The Model

> *Don't you call this a regular jam*
> *I'm gonna rock this land*
> *I'm gonna take this itty-bitty world by storm*
> *And I'm just getting warm*

—J. Smith, M. Williams, G. Clinton, G. Jacobs, J. Mccants,
L. Mccants, S. Stewart, W. Morrison, W. Collins

Remember when MTV played music? And some of it was "unplugged"?

Like so many things in my world, the inspiration for Acoustic Leadership came from music. MTV's *Unplugged*, to be precise.

For many years, starting in 1989, the *Unplugged* sessions were a popular format for the channel. You'd see famous singers and bands from many countries and music genres: Aerosmith, Eric Clapton, LL Cool J, Alanis Morissette, the famous Mexican band, Maná, the Japanese performer Utada Hikaru, and then-new Colombian phenom, Shakira.

Driven by curiosity and a bit of nostalgia, I binge-watched some of those old videos on YouTube. (I did it at work. Don't tell.) I was intrigued. What was it about these performances that made then resonate? Why was the *Unplugged* format so successful for so many years? I thought about this acoustic approach, more from a human psychology standpoint than from a fan or musician perspective, and I noticed three fundamental facets all of the concerts contained that helped drive the appeal:

- *Simplicity*: They were scaled-back, minimalistic, back to the roots of the music. They sounded good. Uncluttered.

- *Authenticity*: The massive production of the arena stages was gone. These were intimate performances: the artists couldn't hide behind effects, multimedia, light shows. They were raw and exposed.

- *Opportunity*: It was a chance to hear (and perform) things in a different way and for the audience to see their favorite artists and familiar tunes in a new light. A chance to unplug, reset, reconnect.

And it all made sense.

Simplicity.

Authenticity.

Opportunity.

Acoustic. Resonant.

There was an approach that I felt could help leaders. That was the focus that was lacking. And not just at my company; I thought that this was the approach that could uncomplicate the leadership puzzle and make a difference at organizations of all sizes, shapes, and locations, be it Coca-Cola or John Deere, Alibaba or Nissan, across the globe or in your company or community.

And Acoustic Leadership was born.

▶ Playlist

Title	Artist	Time
Mama Said Knock You Out	LL Cool J; written by J. Smith, M. Williams, G. Clinton, G. Jacobs, J. Mccants, L. Mccants, S. Stewart, W. Morrison, W. Collins (Def Jam Recordings, 1990).	4:53
Sweet Emotion	Aerosmith; written by S. Tyler and T. Hamilton (Columbia, 1975).	4:34
Head Over Feet	Alanis Morissette; written by A. Morissette and G. Ballard (Maverick/Reprise, 1995).	4:25
Oye Mi Amor	Maná; written by F. Olvera, A. González (WEA Latina, 1992).	4:23
First Love	Utada Hikaru; written by U. Hikaru (Toshiba EMI, 1999).	4:17
Whenever, Wherever	Shakira; written by S. Mebarak, T. Mitchell, G. Estefan (Epic, 2001).	3:16

Visit ricklozano.com/resources for the complete Acoustic Leadership playlist.

The Journey
(Technically Speaking)

> *Tumble out of bed and I stumble to the kitchen*
> *Pour myself a cup of ambition*
> *Yawn and stretch and try to come to life*

—**D. Parton**

We've all been there. Up in the morning, facing a new day, summoning caffeinated courage as we get ready to work nine to five as Dolly Parton so wonderfully sang in 1980. Trying to get by, survive, get our fair shake, and a fighting chance. I suspect that for many of us, that refrain may yet sound familiar in the year 2050.

At the heart of those lyrics is the struggle. Someone is trying to do the right thing. Trying to get ahead. (But the boss won't seem to let them.) Trying to do good work and earn the recognition they feel they deserve. You can probably relate.

We must start with this central idea for the sake of our conversation: People *want* to do great work.

They do! The vast majority of us show up every day, virtually or in person, trying to do the right thing, trying to do good work, hoping for a chance to do better, be better, and get a leg up.

No one comes to work to be awful at their jobs! You might argue that some people *are* horrible — but that was probably not the intention with which they arrived that day. ("It's Tuesday, time-to-suck day!" Who does that?)

People want to build, create cool things, sell new products, do right by customers, make money. People want to feel a sense of pride in what they do, where they and with whom they do it.

People want to do great work. Are you helping them?

Or are you getting in the way?

Much research has come out over the last decade and a half specifically about motivations in the workplace. We've seen changing expectations and desires of the new workforce, what people want and are motivated by — and it is worth delving into.

Daniel Pink's book, *Drive: The Surprising Truth About What Motivates Us* is particularly enlightening: the traditional carrot-and-stick motivation model — perks for performance, punishments for lack of it — doesn't work as effectively as it used to. (Did it ever really?) The traditional motivators of human behavior at work — money and other structural incentives as the carrot, penalties as the stick — aren't the ultimate movers we always thought they were. In this new world, Pink argues, money still matters, but it isn't the *only* thing that matters. People are more interested in other things: autonomy, mastery, and purpose. If proffered and cultivated appropriately, these three areas can be leveraged and used to engender better work and natural motivation, more so than the nominal gains of a slight pay raise. And these fundamental offerings seemed to be the exact thematic difference prominently popping up in the realms of technology, engagement, and leadership: the melody of each individual was sweeter, so the harmonies created by the whole were more robust and cohesive.

For a significant number of corporate refugees over the last few decades, the technology sector provided a welcome and stark contrast to the buttoned-up corporate world. I witnessed this firsthand; when I stepped foot into the tech space in 2010, I immediately realized my new surroundings were a far cry from the norms I was used to after spending the previous decade in the corporate world of financial services. I had joined Rackspace Hosting, now Rackspace Technology, an internet hosting and cloud computing company growing at light speed. I quickly traded in my suit and tie uniform for a dozen T-shirts and a few pairs of jeans, and it felt good. I belonged here; I was home!

And it wasn't just me. The tech space was buzzing all over the world, experiencing an influx in job applications and garnering acclaim in multiple "Great Places to Work" lists.

What was it about these technology company settings that seemed so compelling to so many people, so reinvigorating and fresh? Why were team members so happy compared to other places and other industries? Why did work seem so...fun?

Employees were intrinsically motivated. Even frontline staff seemed to have more ownership, more empowerment, more choices over how and when they did their work. More autonomy. And they weren't just workers; they were fans, enthusiastically in love with the place. There was a buzz, this feeling of real community, the idea that this evolving array of cloud technology would democratize computing and change the world. There was this shared purpose, a collective identity. People were growing and learning and building, and it felt great. And they loved their leaders; the executive team members were practically celebrities.

Even this ideal world, however, wasn't perfect and without fault by any means. (And, of course, this was a single point in time. All company cultures change.) But it was, indeed, a unique and vibrant time and culture, and it helps us point to the many connections between engagement, organizational design, and leadership since so many of the examples of compelling work cultures come, in significant numbers, from the tech world.

That said, consider this:

| Technology companies don't own the market on engagement. They didn't then, and they don't now.

Want proof? Pull up the various "Great Places to Work" lists again, and you will find plenty of other companies that have nothing to do with tech yet are still serial achievers: the grocery stores Wegmans and Publix, the Cheesecake Factory, insurance companies, biotech firms, hotels. These organizations are also doing great things, creating dynamic environments where people want to work. Each in its different way, sure, and these are just a few examples that illustrate that an engaging culture is possible in many industries.

Of course, the point was that in every case, in every industry, leaders directly impacted the culture. They were a big part of how people felt about work. Leaders such as the Arne Sorenson at Marriott, Dan Price at Gravity Payments, Tony Hsieh at Zappos, Beth Ford at Land O' Lakes – these influential figures inspired loyalty, raving fans, and drove incredible business value at the same time.

But the question remained: *why were so many of them tech companies?* They sure made up a vast portion of the brands represented. Were there inherent advantages in the tech space that weren't, in fact, repeatable in other industries?

When you look closer, you can identify two things contributing to tech firms' prevalence on these lists. And they had to do with this idea of startup culture.

Start me up.

What qualifies as a startup?

There are differing schools of thought on this one. Some insist they are the bootstrapping outfits that litter the Bay Area/Silicon Valley and other emerging tech hubs worldwide. Others say it still includes the behemoths like Facebook and Google. Others insist a startup is merely a mindset, a mentality.

As Eric Reis, author of *The Lean Startup: How Today's Entrepreneurs Use Continuous Innovation to Create Radically Successful Business*, defines it, a "startup is a human institution designed to create a new product or service under conditions of extreme uncertainty."

Okay. By that definition, both big tech companies and smaller ones could qualify as a startup. (For that matter, most small businesses, including my Unlock & Amplify movement, could be eligible under that definition, but we'll keep it simple and focus on tech for the moment.) Upon further reflection, a simple logistical element emerges from the nature of that definition and that environment: "conditions of extreme uncertainty." As drivers of culture and human behavior, "conditions of extreme uncertainty" produce an unintended (perhaps) outcome: extensions of empowerment, ownership, and autonomy that weren't entirely intentional or by design.

Operating under conditions of uncertainty, especially for a tech company, means keeping up with the lightning speed of technology leapfrogs, fighting continuous bugs and cyberattacks, all without a guarantee of funding or an imminent buyout from a predator company. Yeah, that might change people's behavior.

Tech companies in the early days of cloud computing were dealing with just that. Another market shift accompanied every day, a different valuation and assessment of the organization, a new reorg to align with how sales and support were changing to meet customers' needs. Time was of the essence; indecision was perilous, stagnancy was a death sentence. They had to *move!*

Candidly put, the issue was being forced. Ownership and empowerment were less a deliberate opportunity thoughtfully given by leaders to their teams and more a requirement based on scarce resources and urgency. (Not always the case, but it is short-sighted to assume it was the altruistic graces of a leader that were helping in these cases.) In many scenarios, the leaders were also the founders, creators, engineers, and customer service reps. Employees at all levels owned things because, in many circumstances, they *had* to.

But here's the thing: regardless of the underpinnings, it resonated with and motivated employees in these companies. Bain & Company looked at several tech firms, Apple, IBM, Dell, and others, and found that employees in these organizations were 40 percent more productive than the average. And, most strikingly, that percentage of productivity shot up to a whopping 125 percent when they reported to an "inspiring" boss.

A second realization about startup culture was that, yes, it did have a lot to do with size. Startups were less hierarchical, flatter organizationally, and the smaller population's very nature impacted the perception of bureaucracy, politics, and red tape. Data published in a *Harvard Business Review* study showed that, in most cases, the smaller the company size, the higher the employee engagement numbers. The very nature of being smaller made it easier to get stuff done.

So, what is the take-away here? That the engaged cultures and the leaders in these examples were accidental and can't be replicated? Not entirely. While there might have been a different driving source of influence that forced the issue in some of these cases, and yes, the tech space contains countless stories of fun work environments that included beer kegs, catered lunches, and ping pong tables, that wasn't the main attraction.

| Someone will only find an original Donkey Kong video game in the breakroom a "perk" for so long.

(Three months and six days to be exact. Don't ask how I know this.)

Rather, the magic was in the emotional connections and psychological commitments these cultures afforded. People felt empowered and owned their work. Personal identities were tied into and aligned with the company. Teams were able to produce, build, move, and their leaders helped them do so. They fostered a feeling of possibility, of creation, perhaps akin to the wonder a songwriter feels when their emotions spring into fruition.

Which brings us to Acoustic Leadership's next core idea.

▶ Playlist

Title	Artist	Time
9 to 5	Dolly Parton; written by D. Parton (RCA Nashville, 1980).	2:42
Start Me Up	The Rolling Stones; written by M. Jagger and K. Richards (Rolling Stones, 1981).	3:33

Visit ricklozano.com/resources for the complete Acoustic Leadership playlist.

The Muck

> Across the alley from the Alamo
> When the starlight beams its tender glow
> the beams go to sleep and then there ain't no dough
> For the people passing by

—J. Greene

People want to get shit done. (#truth.)

I'd say that over coffee or cocktails and it is important to stress as we enter the next phase of our discussion. People want to rock at their jobs.

| Don't strand your key talent at the intersection of ambition and helplessness.

They — and *you* — are motivated to do great work, and nothing feels worse than realizing your hands are tied, ultimately feeling like your leader is getting in the way of your getting things done. So, what gets in the way?

Take a walk with me, and we'll find one answer in my hometown, San Antonio. (Cue "Across The Alley From The Alamo," cited above. I love the Mills Brothers' classic version.)

In actuality, across the alley from the Alamo, there's a couple of tourist trap destinations vying for your attention (and money), but down below street level, accessible from numerous locations, is the San Antonio Riverwalk. It is pretty sweet these days, too. The city of San Antonio has done an incredible job of reinventing the Riverwalk. They have cleaned it up, built it out, extended it further north and south. You'll find the hip Pearl Brewery area to the north, which you have to check out next time you are here. It is a splendid space, and the remains of the original Pearl Brewery building are now the chic Hotel Emma — and it is fantastic!

Further south, the "Mission Reach" extends to the outskirts of downtown. It has a vast stretch of jogging/walking/biking trails, and if you go even further down that way, you'll find several well-preserved missions that are much larger and more impressive (and with less death) than the Alamo. Mission Espada is remarkably serene.

At least once a year, the city dams up the locks at the north end of the river and drains the whole thing dry. All that is left is a soggy riverbed of muck, algae, empty cans, the occasional tennis shoe, engagement rings…a dead body. (That might be an exaggeration. Might be.)

Crews fan out along the length of the river and do their job fixing the edges of the walkway, scrubbing the walls, repainting, getting rid of the muck so that the river flows smoother, quicker, cleaner, and entices tourists to spend their hard-earned dollars below street level. (Pro tip: if you are the foodie type, don't limit your culinary exploration to the Riverwalk. San Antonio has a vast number of truly excellent food options!)

And that, dear reader, brings us back to your role and tees up our next question.

▌ What the muck?

That's right, what the muck?

Are we making it simple for people to get things done? Not always.

Sometimes we are creating just that: muck. Things that get in the way. Sludge that slows us down, stops us in our tracks, limits flow and creativity, puts up unnecessary barriers, and impedes progress.

Every organization has some level of muck. Some leaders create muck, and others alleviate it. Some do both without realizing it. Sometimes we, the leaders, *are* the muck.

So, to make it simple for people to do their best work, ask yourself this vital question again, "What the muck?"

And when you find the muck, eliminate it. (That sounds like something the Terminator would say.)

Some might argue that the least amount of muck exists back in that startup world, benefiting from the luxury of small teams and fewer actors. But startups grow, get sold, or die. At any rate, they change. The size of the company, the scope of the work, the people, everything evolves, and that (except the die option) is usually a good thing. It means the company is on the right track. For some founders, the whole objective is to grow enough to sell the company at a hefty profit.

Startups scale. They evolve. Or they disappear. (What will yours do?)

And though evolution is generally good, that doesn't eliminate challenges. Often, when companies scale, even the most revered cultural icons can become rusty relics of days gone by, and not everyone will agree with the direction the company goes and the choices made. For example, when Google's Chief Executive Officer Sundar Pichai announced that the company was changing the format of the longstanding weekly all-hands meeting known as "TGIF," it bothered some Googlers. TGIFs were sacred! Nevertheless, various factors led to the discussions changing from a weekly to a monthly schedule. Additionally, the format itself evolved from a Q-and-A-type session to a more formal presentation focused only on business and strategy updates. Some Googlers questioned if the transparency they valued was a thing of the past; they publicly mourned the loss of a cornerstone of their cultural identity and cited an unwelcome shift from their core values.

But Pichai's reasons for the change made sense, at least on paper. He described "a coordinated effort to share our conversations outside of the company after every TGIF" and claimed that those efforts "affected our ability to use TGIF as a forum for candid conversations on important topics." In other words, the transparent, candid conversations that Googlers loved could only exist if they committed to confidentiality, to "keeping it in the room." And it wasn't always happening.

Another reason for the change was that people weren't showing up. A weekly event that used to attract 80 percent attendance had dwindled to a meager 25 percent. As the company grew, people became more geographically dispersed, and, as new talent arrived, the TGIF meetings didn't have the same emotional, perhaps nostalgic, connection for recent hires. Googlers were generally still engaging, just not in that particular format. A change was overdue.

As companies evolve, traditions morph, priorities shift, human capital momentum sometimes moves in different directions, and sometimes even the most sacred traditions need to be scrutinized. And sometimes, the things that used to work, the things we used to love, turn into muck.

There are two things every company and every leader needs to know: first, the cultural landscape of every company will continually change over time, like it or not. Second, as companies grow, so does the muck.

Got muck? Yes, you do. Every organization does. To eliminate it, you have to be aware of and acknowledge its existence.

Time for a muck analysis.

(A mucknalysis?)

Bring on the BDIP.
Examining the makeup of muck.

Yes, BDIP, the mnemonic device for the four general categories of muck:

1. **B**ureaucracy
2. **D**inosaurs
3. **I**nfrastructure
4. **P**eople

The case can probably be made for even more categories, and you'll notice that some of the examples could exist or walk the line between all of them, but for the sake of simplicity (more on that in the next chapter), let's stick with these four.

Plus, the phrase "BDIP" is fun.

B-dip.

B-dip.

B-dip, B-dip.

No one wants to be defeated.

"Showin' how funky, strong is your fight, it doesn't matter, who's wrong or right, just BDIP!"

You totally sang it, didn't you?

(And, if for some crazy reason it hasn't connected yet, the tune is the booty-shaking "Beat It" by Michael Jackson. And, yes, you can love the music and not the person.)

Now, let's break down BDIP.

Bureaucracy.

What emotions does that term elicit?

Frustration, perhaps?

In researching the "muck" concept, one word kept surfacing: Bureaucracy.

"Dude, bureaucracy. Try getting anything done here."

"Red tape, bureaucracy, politics, all that crap that drives me nuts…."

In informal conversations with participants in my training sessions, with attendees at a conference I was speaking at, bureaucracy was frequently mentioned. It didn't necessarily rank highest on their frustration list, mind you, it just seemed to be on everyone's lips. So, I did a web search to see if everyone was talking about the same thing.

Bureaucracy, aside from being a difficult word to spell, is:

- A system of government in which most of the important decisions are made by state officials rather than by elected representatives.
- A state or organization governed or managed as a bureaucracy.
- A hierarchy.

And lastly,

- Excessively complicated administrative procedure.

There it is, "Excessively complicated administrative procedure." Complicated: the opposite of simple. Are you making things complicated? According to the data, yes.

And we have been doing it for a while.

In 2017 the *Harvard Business Review* published an incredibly insightful article titled "What We Learned about Bureaucracy from 7,000 HBR Readers" by Gary Hamel and Michele Zanini, and it has a big story to tell. Using what they called their Bureaucracy Mass Index tool (BMI), they asked respondents to gauge the extent to which bureaucracy was prevalent in their company or organization. The results were astounding but probably not all that surprising. To summarize:

- It is generally everywhere. Every organization has some form of it.
- It is getting worse.
- It impedes speed and innovation. (No surprise.)
- It drains the soul and life out of people.

Okay, that last one was my addition, but bureaucracy always leads to feelings of disempowerment and frustration. Read the article for yourself and see what you think and how this plays out in your company.

Open your internet browser of choice and type in "What We Learned about Bureaucracy from 7,000 HBR Readers" by Gary Hamel and Michele Zanini.

Do it now.

Seriously.

It will take you five minutes to read. You've got the time.

Then, come back with your observations.

Hi there.

Welcome back. ("How you doin?")

Interesting, huh? What did you think about these highlights?

- Size, indeed, matters. The larger the company, the more likely the respondents were to feel bureaucratic muck. And it isn't just size; it is layers. Companies aren't getting "flatter," in fact, most frontline employees have eight hierarchical management layers above them.

- Again, it's getting worse! How is this possible? With over five million sixty-one thousand ideas on leadership, business, and organizational development, how do we not know that bureaucracy is the muck equivalent of cement or quicksand? Why haven't we done more to stop it? But there it was: nearly two-thirds of the respondents said they felt things trending in a muck-like direction. Only 13 percent indicated that they had seen improvement.

- And the biggest surprise: the job function category reporting the highest increase in bureaucracy. Any guesses what it might be? An astounding 74 percent of people identified as working in *customer service* said their org had grown more bureaucratic over the last few years.

Customer service! Isn't this the absolute last place you want muck? The function that directly serves — and is responsible for gaining or losing — your customers?

Consider what that muck sounds like to a customer; no doubt you've experienced it:

"Sorry, that's just our policy."

"That's the standard procedure we have to follow."

"I'd have to get another layer of approval for that."

"My manager won't let me."

How do those phrases make you feel?

Sure, you *could* directly blame the person saying those words, especially if the customer service was accompanied by an "I don't get paid enough to put up with this" attitude. But what if the words out of their mouths are telling a bigger story? What if this utterance is a reflection of how *they* feel? Disempowered. Hands tied. Deflated and conveying the message: "I've tried before, and every time I did, I got yelled at, so I'm not even going to bother." Maybe their words were a "Tale of Bureaucracy," in the form of policies, procedures, and politics, perhaps with the spectre of an overbearing and intimidating supervisor.

This person either can't or isn't able to do a great job either way.

Muck, muck, muck.

When Mary Barra first became vice president of human resources at General Motors in 2009, she immediately faced a muck monster. GM had recently filed for bankruptcy. They were desperately trying to figure out a way forward, and Mary realized that for the company to navigate mucky waters as quickly as possible, they had to analyze *everything* that was preventing GM employees from doing their best work. She started with what might seem to be the most inconsequential item, the company dress code.

Which was 10 pages long.

Seriously?

1. What could possibly take 10 pages to describe in a dress code?
2. What message are companies like this sending?

Ten pages of instruction? Ten pages of detailed criteria that people had to understand and agree to — just to show up for work? Wasting everyone's time and energy with 10 pages of rules — only to walk in the door? Absurd!

Something wasn't right.

Mary, who has since gone on to become CEO, decided to do something about it. She took the comprehensive policy in place and reduced it down to two words, "Dress appropriately." Two words instead of 10 pages. Done.

Except it wasn't. The change wasn't easy. Skepticism within her business unit abounded. One leader argued that some GM employees regularly meet with government officials. Didn't they need an official protocol to cover that?

She encouraged that leader to take it to the team to discuss and solve. They decided that those employees who had to meet with the government officials would keep an extra pair of dress clothes in their locker for use when needed. Simple as that. No need to write more words in the policy.

According to an article in *Quartz at Work*, Mary puts it this way,

> *What I realized is that you really need to make sure your managers are empowered — because if they cannot handle "dress appropriately," what other decisions can they handle? And I realized that often, if you have a lot of overly prescriptive policies and procedures, people will live down to them....*
>
> *But if you let people own policies themselves, especially at the first level of people supervision, it helps develop them. It was an eye-opening experience, but I now know that these small little things changed our culture powerfully. They weren't the only factor, but they contributed significantly.*

Don't you love that approach? Not only does it abolish muck, but it helps the first-level leaders develop. Rather than punting the issue to HR or escalating the problem, they must own the situation and resolve it. Like she said, if they can't handle that, what can they handle?

It was a small change, but it's a great example of where we all need to start.

What are the immediate things in our sphere of control that are getting in the way or making it difficult for people to do their best work? Or even show up? Or own it?

Time for us all to become muck-busters.

Dinosaurs.

They ruled the earth. Probably would've been around forever if not for that darned asteroid.

They are long gone now unless you count their distant cousins, like the mugger crocodile in India. Or birds. But these days, dinosaurs are defined as those rituals and processes that refuse to die. Those ways of working that may have served a purpose years ago but, now? Why do those outdated policies and procedures still exist?

We can see that entrenched, archaic thinking when Mary Barra introduced the new dress code: "We've always had a policy. We can't do without a policy. How will people know what to wear?" While it is easy for us to understand how hard it was to kill that dinosaur, and even though we can laugh at it, her colleagues didn't think it was a darn bit funny. They wanted to hang on to their dinosaur, and Barra had to figure out a way to pry it gently out of their hands and let people define how they wanted to stroll down the catwalk.

Sticking to the world of fashion (okay, t-shirts and jeans), when I began at Rackspace, the dress code was also two words: *wear clothes.*

And do you know what? Most people did!

Go figure!

Just as most of us come to work wanting to do a good job (and wanting to wear clothes!), most people can be trusted to do the right thing. All too often, policies and protocols, from what people wear to what people are allowed to spend, are created as an overreaction to a few instances where people made poor decisions — the disruptive outliers. Someone messed up; now everyone pays the price.

Look, this isn't a policy problem; this is a *management* problem, an *accountability* problem.

But the dinosaurs are still here. They roam the halls, taking up much-needed space and oxygen. Flailing their short little *T. rex* arms. (Why is that always funny?) The policies we have because we've always had them. The work processes we do because we've done them forever. The traditions we continue to validate and propagate because...why again?

Do you have a dinosaur at work?

(And why is *dinosaur* so hard a word for me to type? Come on, fingers!)

Can you think of one?

A dinosaur you keep as a pet and continue to feed? There may not be a reason for it, but neither is there a reasonable alternative, so it remains...one of those outdated practices or rules, a ritual that everyone adheres but hates.

Take a moment. Think of one. Everyone will wait.

Have you identified one yet? You have?

Okay. On the count of three, everyone shouts it at the same time. Ready?

One.

Two.

Three.

🦖 "Mandatory compliance training!"

🦖 "Fax machines!"

🦖 "Having to create new PowerPoint decks for every meeting!"

🦖 "Performance reviews!"

Oh. You went *there*. Alrighty then.

Sit tight. Let's talk.

> *I'm writing your performance review*
> *It says more about me than you*
> *It's morally defeating and often misleading*
> *But this is the best we can do*
> — © R. Lozano

This cheeky piece — "The Performance Review Song" — happens to be one of my own, in which I playfully describe what it sounds like when performance reviews go bad. (I haven't recorded it yet, but if you want a laugh, I have included a video of me playing it during one of my keynotes on ricklozano.com/resources. Tell me what you think, and if you're inspired, send me more lyrics and I'll include them in an upcoming keynote!)

Candidly, performance reviews are a divisive subject, and it would have been easy to leave them out of the discussion altogether here in *Acoustic Leadership*. After all, it's likely that most of you reading this book are not in a position to change your company's whole performance review system. Why talk about the things you can't change when we can spend some time talking about the dinosaurs you can tame?

Because this is the *T. rex* of dinosaurs.

And this is just one example of many. We will examine this concept closer in chapter 5, but for now, pretend to be a paleontologist and scrutinize this dinosaur's anatomy.

Performance reviews. The dreaded annual or biannual conversations that typically determine whether or not people get promotions or raises. For many, it's the source of their official employee "rating."

They take up a considerable amount of time, effort, and energy.

Performance reviews are often the source of dread, the cause of worry, and the harbinger of the exquisite annual torture practice known as the *self-evaluation*.

You might be familiar: it's the part of the procedure where you write your own review, distill down the successes you've been carefully documenting over the last year, using wording that makes it sound like you invented the copy machine. (The one that works, though.)

And the development stuff? The requisite "areas of opportunity" you have to bring to light begrudgingly? (Read: all your misses, missteps, mishaps, and mischief.) Well, you are smart. Of course, these are the areas you spin as the things you are doing *well*; you just wish you could do *better*. You publish the positive in bold text and clever wording while diminishing the things that *might* be used against you later.

The self-evaluation. It's the document you spend hours crafting and refining, only to have — in some infuriating cases — your manager ultimately copy and paste your exact words into your official review!

But really, you can't even blame your manager. In many cases, they hate this brontosaurus of bull shit too! It is a ton of work to compile all that data and invest in a process that no one finds valuable! (By the way, have you heard the stories of people whose bosses accidentally cut and pasted someone else's self-evaluation and put it into theirs? It happens! How awkward that would be, "Uh...boss...I noticed in my review that you called me Magdalena.... my name is Dave.")

The performance review process is a prominent example of muck that some consultants somewhere convinced companies everywhere is necessary. And the most incredible thing — despite all the dread, work, time, the foreboding, even the goodwill and best efforts that many leaders put into this — **they don't work.**

Performance reviews don't work!

At least not in motivating performance.

According to one study, 93 percent of companies conduct employee reviews while less than half, 49 percent of those who facilitate the process, believe that performance reviews accurately appraise *performance*. And, by the way, this data is coming from SHRM, the Society for Human Resource Management! So, why do we keep feeding the performance review dinosaur?

To be clear, this is not an attempt to identify any single process or function as the problem. And to be fair, some organizations are having success with their review system, and if it works for them and has the desired results, and — this is important — is helping make it *simple* for people to get their jobs done, fantastic!

It is an effort to create awareness. Only you know what the muck dinosaurs are where you work. Examine carefully those things that might get in the way rather than help. Feel free to delete the stuff you can and modify the things you can't. As Forrest Gump would say, "that's all I have to say about that." For now. Enough with the pterodactyls.

Dinosaurs. They're a type of muck. They get in the way of staff doing their best work. They are the protocols inherited, and maybe no one even knows why. They are the tasks sometimes assigned as busywork. Muck.

Let's hope their fossilized relics don't become part of the...

Infrastructure.

More specifically, the indiscernible infrastructure.

Have you ever been scuba diving? I recommend it, if possible; it is transformational. Newer divers, rightfully, spend most of their time hyper-focused on their breathing, depths, watching their gauges, and occasionally the larger fish (and sharks!) that swim by. More experienced divers, while hopefully following safety protocol, take note of more attractive details: the yellowhead jawfish poking its head up from the seafloor, the juvenile parrotfish population, that invasive lionfish species. (The unfortunate bleaching of coral populations due to climate change...don't get me started.)

But even the most experienced divers often miss, for example, the rarely seen mimic octopus meshing with its coral reef surroundings. It is there, but you wouldn't know it if you aren't carefully looking. You almost didn't see it, but suddenly, there it is! It was always there. Built-in, baked into the infrastructure, imperceptible until it isn't. Divers fortunate to see these fabulous creatures are usually elated, but back at work, we often don't realize the muck meshing with our surroundings. But it is alive and operational, dragging us down, sometimes without even our awareness. The equivalent of, say, malware, getting in the way of our emotional hard drive's optimal performance. (That was deep.)

It's also kind of like a casino. Have you ever been? Casinos are the most ingeniously (and diabolically) designed structures. Everything about them, everything in them, is intended to facilitate two desired actions: stay longer and spend more.

And to accomplish this, there is an array of subtle enablers built into the environment's infrastructure. No clocks, hard-to-find exits, cheap or free drinks (depending on the venue and how much you gamble), ticket-redemption machines strategically placed in the center of the building, so you have to walk by more temptations before you leave. You're surrounded by a gazillion lights, bells, and whistles, reinforcing that you might be the next big winner! You may be broke now, but wait! All these built-in mechanisms drive the primary behavior that the casino values: spending money!

What does *your* organization value? And is its infrastructure, tangible or otherwise, driving those behaviors or enabling the opposite?

Why do people get promoted? How and why are leaders behaving the way they are behaving? And what is the underlying motivator at play?

Earlier I mentioned that the traditional carrot-and-stick approach isn't the only or most effective motivational model in today's world. That does not mean, however, that it doesn't still motivate. It does. People still crave those carrots, often in the form of money and power. Many workers do, indeed, fear the stick when it presents itself in the form of a write-up or the threat of being fired. We are all motivated, to varying degrees, by these things.

But those aren't the only things. And here is where it gets tricky.

Go back to the first question: What does your organization value? Results? It probably does in some form. What metrics are you using to show those results? In the sales world, it is reasonably straightforward: numbers tied to closings, bookings, monthly recurring revenue — all the things that keep your business afloat. But what are most salespersons motivated to sell? The right product for the customer? Or the one that earns them the highest commission?

We have all seen examples of incorrect or inappropriate incentives leading to behaviors that were less than desirable. Leaders are not immune from taking the occasional erroneous path, and a misalignment of structural motivators can lead them to value the wrong behavior and enable potentially harmful outputs that increase the likelihood of muck and disengagement. From Volkswagen to Wells Fargo, we've seen numerous situations recently where the constant pressure for high sales numbers led to actions that weren't in their customers' best interest. (Or legal.)

A few examples of misguided value drivers:

- *Pride*: Afraid of looking bad, management refuses to change course, wasting time and team energy on something that isn't working.
- *Convenience*: Why have a challenging conversation or deal with this at all? Create a policy. Apply it to everyone.
- *Insecurity*: Worried they might make the wrong decision, they make none. And the lack of direction sends people spinning.
- *Winning*: You. Thrown under the bus.
- *Promotions*: This company loves productivity, and the people who advance have numbers. Let's do many things that can show many numbers! Are these important things? Who cares? Look at how many things we do! And forget about accomplishments that don't have a number!

And these are just some prominent examples. Other, often more understated pressures and demands make this a complex muck to realize, much less bust. Are we creating an infrastructure that encourages the desired behaviors from leaders and those they lead?

Perhaps this discussion on infrastructure and structural motivators can help, in part, explain…

People.

The reckoning. (Reread those words with the Star Wars theme song playing in your head.)

Have you ever had a bad manager? The vast majority would say yes.

Have you ever *been* a lousy manager? Maybe just a little?

Most people want to be great at what they do, so why does it happen? Why are there so many horror stories of the boss who drove people insane and ultimately through the exit the door, never to return?

Maybe it is because there are infrastructural dynamics in place that reward certain behaviors, like speed and aggression, while penalizing others, say listening or empathy. Since people take cues from their leaders, a domino effect often occurs wherein people *do* because their leaders *do*. To a certain degree, this combination has led to many and varied types of ineffective leadership approaches from, perhaps, well-intentioned individuals. Let's introduce a few archetypes.

Please note: the following examples are not scientific in nature, nor are they tied to a specific personality, demographic, culture, or style. (Do not try these at home!) They are exaggerated caricatures of leaders misbehaving and making poor choices to illustrate the point. I am sure, however, you will recognize a few of them.

The micromanager approach
Perhaps the most common.

The manager who is all up in your biz, breathing down your neck, not trusting you to do your job (that you are perfectly capable of doing), continually checking up and checking in.

As Tom Petty says in his classic song, "Don't do me like that!"

Everyone hates micromanagement when they feel it, but from a behavioral standpoint, what exactly is it? At its core, micromanagement is a collection of overly directive and involved behaviors that are situationally inappropriate. But why would well-intentioned leaders be overinvolved with someone who doesn't need it? A few possibilities:

- *Control:* Ego, maybe a desire for significance or mistrust in others' abilities combined with fear of how it will reflect on them. They can't let go.
- *Consistency:* Perhaps they are inflexible in their leadership style or are just trying to "treat everyone the same" when treating people accordingly is a better idea.
- *Expedience:* It would be quicker if they just did it themselves — "I used to do this job, that's why I got promoted" — so get out of the way.

It's a funny thing about micromanagers and their collection of directive behaviors that monitor, dictate, structure, and instruct. The actions themselves aren't inherently wrong, just poorly timed. If you think back to the first few weeks of your onboarding, when your boss told you whom to meet, gave you a schedule, and checked in frequently to make sure you were comfortable, you didn't hate those behaviors then.

But, oh, don't those same behaviors make you want to scream when you are working on a task you could do in your sleep?

Tom Petty also sang, "Well, I won't back down," but in this case…please do. Back off. We've got this.

The Micromanager not only drives down morale s/he also makes things harder, and over-involvement often inadvertently makes everything take longer.

Mucho muck.

The climber approach

Ah, they soar higher, but everything below smolders in ashes.

The term "the tragedy of the commons" applies here. It originated as an economic theory that describes a situation where one person, acting in their self-interest, depletes, or ruins a shared resource to benefit themselves.

The term has been used in contemporary scenarios, for example, the destruction of the environment for profit. Whereby, even though we all live on the same planet and share the common resource (air, water, plants), one person/organization's greed or appetite for profit ultimately ruins something for everyone, including themselves.

How does this apply here? Well, you've probably seen this person at work before, sometimes as a leader, sometimes not. They are hungry to move up, gain recognition, get promotions and please those above them. To look good. The structural motivators in place are driving them to behave in ways that are hurting the shared good.

It often plays out as a person promising their team one thing, acting as their advocate during team meetings and one-on-ones, but performing an about-face when pressure exerts itself from above. The classic "yes-man/woman." Regardless of the team's organizational health, the number of projects currently on the table, the climber will say yes to any request thrown their way, even though it might not be urgent. Even though it might not be the team's biggest priority or might prevent the team from working on their biggest priority.

As in the "tragedy of the commons," they also succeed in harming themselves. Acting in this manner, contrary to the common good, they might elevate their status but harm their image in the process. They will likely erode trust. They set teams up for failure and unwittingly set themselves up for failure as well. Their unwillingness to negotiate or provide a politically savvy "No" comes at a cost and, even though they may climb the ladder, they scar their brand.

They become or have created the muck.

The firefighter approach
All smoke means fire.

A colleague of mine once said of their manager, "How am I ever supposed to do my job when we change direction every damn week in every new meeting?"

Indeed, there had been quite a shift from the previous week's meeting, and it was becoming a disturbing pattern. "We literally agree on everything, walk out of the meeting, and then every time he comes out of one of his meetings, he completely changes focus. Every person he talks to, the thing they talk about is urgent and has to be done now. Give me just one freaking month to focus on my current priority, will you?"

Which structural motivators were in play here? Could it be that the leader felt pressure from above and below (like a fire) and was, perhaps, insecure and unwilling to say no? Maybe they just weren't able to distinguish between urgent and essential, but either way, it didn't matter; the damage had been done. This same colleague was similarly frustrated with her manager assigning time-wasting tasks that weren't necessarily her team's biggest priorities, a common complaint when the whole team does nothing but put out preventable fires.

On the other hand, sophisticated leaders understand that the "tyranny of the urgent" is a powerful force that has to be reckoned with. They realize the potential of wasted time and energy; they know employee buy-in and morale are on the line; they pause, think, and act accordingly. They know that an instant change of direction isn't always needed, and sometimes things aren't on fire. Sometimes that smoke is coming from a delicious, slow-cooking barbeque.

All of this muck costs money.

BDIP: bureaucracy, dinosaurs, infrastructure, and people.

These are some of the familiar forms muck regularly takes. They are all related, and often more than one may be in play, though not everything is a problem everywhere.

But a discussion about muck is worth your time. And your money.

For those of you for whom money is a powerful structural motivator, let's take a deeper look. Leaders directly impact creating engaging work environments, and so much data suggests that engagement matters. But how much, exactly? Well, at Best Buy, about a hundred thousand dollars. Yes, a hundred thousand. And with a minimal amount of work, too! Best Buy studied its analytics and realized that, in one particular store, a 0.1 percent increase in employee engagement directly correlated to a value of over a hundred thousand dollars!

Just 0.1 percent. Even the smallest amount of muck-bustin' is worth a hundred grand!

Time is money. We hear that a lot, but consider these two startling stats:

1. In an article titled "The Three Trillion Dollar Prize for Busting Bureaucracy," Gary Hamel and Michele Zanini of Management Lab put forth compelling evidence suggesting that up to 50 percent of all internal compliance activity (read: muck) is of questionable value, at best. If that were true, then according to their research, that would result in 16 percent of employee time devoted to internal compliance that is "nonproductive."

2. Bain & Company estimates that, due to all of these muckish factors we are discussing, the average company loses 25 percent of its productive power. Shocking.

So, what are your options?

We'll explore them in the coming sections but keep this in mind: if you are spending too much time doing things that aren't valuable, you will likely find yourself eroding employee engagement. In effect, you are getting in the way of people's ability and desire to do great work. You are wasting time and energy, and it costs more than just money.

Time to bust a muck move.

Time to get the muck out.

▶ Playlist

Title	Artist	Time
Across the Alley from The Alamo	The Mills Brothers; written by J. Greene (Decca, 1947).	2:10
Beat It	Michael Jackson; written by M. Jackson (Epic, 1982).	4:18
The Performance Review Song	Rick Lozano; written by R. Lozano (YouTube (https://www.youtube.com/watch?v=a1-MLy88he4), 2017).	1:30
Don't Do Me Like That	Tom Petty & The Heartbreakers; written by T. Petty (Backstreet/UME 1979).	2:42
I Won't Back Down	Tom Petty; written by T. Petty and J. Lynn (MCA, 1989).	2:58
Bust a Move	Young MC; written by M. Young, M. Dike, M. Ross (Delicious Vinyl, 1989).	4:24

Visit ricklozano.com/resources for the complete Acoustic Leadership playlist.

II. The Solution

To get over get better, try to be the possessor
Of the one thing we all need in life
To succeed take my advice
Get the knowledge that you really want

—J. Jackson, T. Lewis, J. Harris

Simplicity

> *The hardest thing for me*
> *Is true simplicity*
> *But it's the only thing that's good enough for you*

—T. Curry, B. Babbitt, C. Collins

Out with thee, evil muck!

Now, where to begin?

A well-formed question is usually a great starting point. What do *your people* feel is getting in the way of their best work? Ask the question. Listen. Evaluate. Act. Let's go even further in our quest for muck reduction with your first Amplified Idea.

Amplified Idea

The muck meeting.

Once you are familiar with the muck concepts and have made your way through the rest of this manuscript, you will more than likely be excited and ready to begin implementing Acoustic Leadership. A muck meeting is your first step. Your team's opportunity to have an open and honest discussion around one core question – *what is getting in the way of people doing their best work?*

You may decide to educate your team on the BDIP examples we introduced earlier, or you may begin by just asking that question and listening to their responses. Either way, move the conversation forward in a positive, productive manner and remember, *you are there to help*. What is preventing people from doing their best work?

If your team members are the muck source, it is more practical and disarming to highlight the *behaviors* that make it difficult for people to thrive in their roles, rather than assigning fault to the individual. And it is of the utmost importance to make the environment safe (more on that later) for people to express opinions that differ from yours.

Consider the following during the meeting:

- What work processes slow things down or drain people's energy. Are they still relevant? Are they even needed?
- Examine the legacy or traditional activities you may have inherited. Do they still serve your people and the organization well?
- Where are you spending your time, and is it worth it? Download a time-value tracker off the internet (there are plenty), or just facilitate a discussion on what items are consuming your time versus their relative worth.
- Scrutinize behaviors that have hurt performance or morale. Are they the result of a misaligned motivator? How can you realign?

You'll have access to several more ideas in the following pages to help your muck meeting be even more effective but remember this key point: this meeting's desired outcome is to pinpoint at least one concrete muck item and immediately address it by modifying the muck's nature or eliminating it altogether.

For additional inspiration, look outside your organization as well. I hear more and more stories of people and companies from different industries challenging the status quo and transforming muck into organizational gold.

We'll look across the world to see what others are doing in the coming pages, but for now, a lesson in sound and music recording.

Compress for success.

From Liz Phair's music to Lizzo's, Lil' Wayne to Los Lobos, compression is the key.

It probably comes as no surprise, but most of the music you listen to sounds nothing like the original performance. Today's sophisticated recording technologies, even for simple home studios like mine, take advantage of numerous processing applications that shape and morph every aspect of the sound. These digital audio workstations (DAWs, in recording vernacular) take the original sound source and elevate it to an almost superhero version of itself, a sound that it couldn't achieve naturally. Sometimes the DAW itself is the sound source, using virtual instruments instead of physical ones.

With rare exceptions, every musical work you listen to has an element of compression. In its simplest terms, compression reduces the dynamic range between the softest and loudest sounds in a recording. It "squishes" the sounds together so that a gentle, acoustic guitar sits right in the mix with a thunderous drum kit and a howling singer.

In most cases, when used appropriately, compression makes recordings sound better. It is a ubiquitous tool for producing great-sounding recordings.

What helpful tip can we take away from our discussion of compression? In a word... flatten.

In leadership terms, "flattening" means minimizing the distance between someone's efforts and their ability to produce great work.

Flattening might be interpreted and acted upon in different ways; sometimes, it simply means getting rid of excessive and unnecessary layers.

Zappos, well known for their engaging organizational culture (and shoes!), is an oft-cited employer of flattening techniques through their use of a concept known as Holacracy. At its core, Holacracy is an attempt to invert the typical top-down power structure present in most hierarchies to give people the tools they need to thrive and empower them when they need it most.

Instead of a complex, multi-layered management system, Zappos relies on self-management and team "circles" empowered with decision-making power. An ever-evolving form of the Holacracy concept has been in place since 2012 at Zappos, and still, they admit that there have been changes since then. As you might imagine, such a movement has its share of fans, detractors, and doubters. Some suspect they are moving away from some of the ideas altogether, while still other companies, such as Boldare, a digital design company in Poland, have decided to adopt Holacracy. (Zappos acknowledges it has evolved within the model but makes no externally-facing mention of abandoning the movement.)

The point is that many organizations continue to challenge the traditional layout of companies in an attempt to *flatten*; in other words, to minimize the layers and obstacles to productivity and engagement.

Before we continue, let me reiterate a key fact here: I understand that most of you are not in a position to reinvent the way your organizations are formed and operate. However, these examples can be used as conceptual fodder to nourish immediate tactical and practical adjustments at any level of your organization.

In the spirit of igniting interest in the possibilities, let's explore an illustration of innovation in the unlikeliest of places — banking. ("Really?" Yes, really. Banks constantly innovate products and the way they serve customers, but not usually their organizational structure.)

Svenska Handelsbanken is a Swedish bank, the oldest on the Swedish stock exchange, with more than eight hundred locations spread across Europe and the UK. In the 1970s, they removed middle management layers and gave each local branch control and power and the authority to make their own decisions for how they operate their business.

Even more pertinent to this discussion, their self-described "trust-based way of working" gives employees the "responsibility and power to decide on questions closest to them." At a local level, people are empowered, encouraged, and expected to act like owners and are given a genuine sense of ownership in their work. Because they are owners; if they meet their goals and certain specific preconditions, every employee gets an equal share of the profits in the form of shares. As a result, employees are one of the bank's largest shareholders.

More amazingly, in a company with over twelve thousand employees, there are only three levels! In a bank! And they've been doing it — quite successfully — for decades!

If a large bank can reduce the muck, empower their talent, and make it simple for people to do their best work, what excuse do you have?

Let's try something new, shall we? Let's make pancakes!

Flatcakes, even.

Per our previous discussion and the Svenska example, the question becomes how do you stay lean, nimble, and flat, startup-style?

How do you give people that sense of autonomy and ownership, that ability to directly, immediately, *simply* make their own decisions and do their best work?

✳ One practical way is to remove excess layers of required approval. Eliminate the policies that don't make sense, and then solve for the exception. Send back to the Mesozoic Era all the dinosaur work that no one is quite sure why you still do in the first place, all those things that taste of muckish red tape and bureaucracy. That, you can do.

I'll provide further examples that will illuminate what opportunities lie in front of you and your team and encourage you to take action, but first, I have good news.

You've earned a promotion!

Congratulations!

I realized that if I'm asking people to behave differently, I need to take my own advice and give you the authority and, in this case, job title — to truly own the task at hand. It is a slight shift, but one that you might have commonly seen in the tech world, where people got creative with their job titles to reflect not only their work but also the work they aspire to bring to fruition. You may have seen them: Customer Service Ninja, Ambassador of Buzz, Chief Amazement Officer, Sales Yoda, Product Evangelist.

I remember hearing a radio story about the trend a few years back. It had become increasingly common in Silicon Valley. The people interviewed for the piece said that the freedom to "call it what you want" lent itself to a feeling of power, pride, and subsequently to a change in behavior. That autonomy thing again. Theoretically, at least, a shift in mindset from Marketing Consultant IV to Ambassador of Buzz taps into the confidence of a stage-diving punk rocker. (Do carefully think it through before you go updating your job title on your resume, however. My recruiter friends have mentioned that some applicant tracking systems can pass on your application entirely if you don't have a specific set of words in your job title during the automated prescreening process. "Marketing," for example, in the previous situation.)

In any case, congratulations again! You have now earned your new job title: CMB.

Chief Muck Buster.

And your people love you. One reason? Because you…

Ac-cent-tchu-ate the positive.

E-li-mi-nate the negative.

Numerous versions of "Ac-cent-tchu-ate The Positive" have been performed throughout the years, but Ella Fitzgerald's is my favorite. What a voice! One of those timeless and singular styles that have entertained thousands for decades.

Hey, right now is the perfect time to stop and listen to a little Ella.

(Ella break. If you want to get even more joy, listen to Ella and Louis Armstrong together!)

Okay, back to work. Your new role. It's onboarding time.

If you want people to perform well in their role and exhibit the behaviors that your company values and ingrain them in your leadership culture, you have to give them explicit information about what those behaviors are. Immediately. And provide an opportunity to practice. Knowing isn't enough.

Let's start with an understanding of what your new role requires. Your central purpose, as CMB, is to get rid of the muck. Eliminate (the negative), modify it, renegotiate it. Do a site survey of what exists, make informed choices where you can, and get out your muck-dusting brush.

Now, the application.

It's time for a good ole policy purge! Yeehaw!

Hang with me.

What stupid rule would you most like to kill? That's the question Warren Berger asks in his book, *The Book of Beautiful Questions*. He says that asking a great question like this (and many others) can help leaders prioritize their activities and assess where to spend their time most efficiently.

What policies, processes, and layers can be eliminated? Today. What would happen if you simply stopped? Even for a little while, as a test? You might be amazed at what you find. Here are some common indicators of possible muck to evaluate/eliminate:

- Everyone hates it, whatever it is. Smells like muck.
- "We've always done it." That's just the policy. "We don't even really know why." (*T. rex* alert!)
- A policy applies to few but affects many.
- A process exists as a direct response to something huge that happened — once.
- "I have people do this because it makes me feel good. I worry too much if I don't know what they are doing."

These are just starting points. I will not go so far as to tell you precisely what you need to cut since every situation is different. And, of course, if a particular policy or protocol makes sense —those that keep people alive, for example — you shouldn't get rid of those! That would be ludicrous.

But the rest?

You'd be surprised at how even the smallest number of unnecessary things, eliminated or tweaked, can make a huge difference, both in simplifying workstreams and in helping people feel valued and empowered. For businesses moving at light-speed that need to innovate fast, it is the difference between Fortune 500 and bankruptcy.

Netflix knows this. The "Netflix Manifesto," as it is known, was originally a slide deck (the "Culture Deck") that laid out the kind of company and leadership culture they were trying to build. It focuses on getting the results Netflix needed by valuing people over process. By encouraging independent decision-making and empowering people to use their skills and talents to serve the greater good. One great example in the Manifesto was their expense policy:

"Our policy for travel, entertainment, gifts, and other expenses is five words long. 'Act in Netflix's best interest.'"

Stunning. That is, indeed, different than most companies.

The current Netflix website does not explicitly refer to the Culture Deck/Manifesto, but the language reinforces the same essential ideas. People first: people over process, independent decision-making, and #5 on the "What is special about Netflix" list:

"Avoid rules."

And instead, trust.

I'm inspired.

Amplified Idea

Conduct a policy purge.

Create a list of all policies and processes, however formal, big, or small, and scrutinize them. What can be modified, automated, delegated, eliminated, or negotiated? What would you be okay without? If you want even more *processus flatinus*, cut the number of processes in half.

Consider the following criteria:

Good process

- Enables your talent to get the best results.
- Aids in communication without creating unnecessary work.
- Sets guidelines that eliminate the need for additional approvals
- Frees up space and time rather than constraining it.
- Gives people decision-making authority in the right circumstance.

Bad process

- Involves more people than are needed.
- Includes managers when it doesn't have to and without a clear benefit.
- Creates non value-add work.
- Demoralizes, infantilizes, and slows down your key talent.
- Solves for the rare exceptions while sending the signal that people are not to be trusted.

Many teams will leap into action and quickly identify a few pressing opportunities; they may even be excited to inform you of processes *that include you* that they would love to remove. Don't take it personally. Instead, know that you are helping remove a part of the process that may have long been considered a pain in the…

Accentuate the positive, eliminate the negative. And, as with most things, it is always…

A matter of trust.

Trust is everything.

Stephen M.R. Covey has a thing or two to say about it in his book, *The Speed of Trust: The One Thing that Changes Everything.* In it, he introduces 13 behaviors to help build what he deems "relationship trust." The very last of Covey's 13 trust-building behaviors is my favorite. In the Acoustic Leadership model, it weaves its way between all three foundations: simplicity, authenticity, and opportunity. That behavior is to extend trust.

| Do you want to build trust? Give it.

Spotify shines when it comes to this. The organization, which began in Sweden in 2008, revolutionized the way music is shared, listened to, and distributed. (Currently playing "Bang! Bang!" by Dizzy Gillespie.)

Note: as the music industry continues to evolve, musicians and songwriters have paid the price for this streaming convenience. The best way you can ensure that your favorite bands and musicians can continue to do what they do for a living is to attend their live performances and BUY something of theirs, hopefully directly from them or on some online forum such as the current Patreon platform. The money that they make from streaming services is dismal. Unless you are Taylor Swift.

Where was I?

Oh yeah, Spotify.

Spotify has a considerable bias against hierarchy and bureaucracy and demonstrates trust in several ways, including how and when people take time off.

Did you ever have a boss ask for a doctor's note to prove you were sick? Or worse yet, a death certificate to prove someone died when you legitimately take your bereavement leave? These are illustrations of a gigantic lack of trust.

Look, if you believe that someone is taking advantage of a situation, that is an accountability issue that probably didn't begin or end with them saying they had strep throat and couldn't come in. You are dealing with adults. Don't treat them like children. Hold the people accountable who need to be held liable, and don't insult the rest! More on that later. For now, back to trust.

As a global organization that currently employs residents of more than 90 different nations, Spotify came to realize that not everyone's observed or preferred holiday (religious, cultural, or otherwise) matched the country's holiday schedule where their headquarters was located. In keeping with their culture and values, a large part of which celebrates diversity and inclusion, they decided to implement their Flexible Public Holiday program. The new arrangement allows employees to work on a locally observed holiday and, in exchange, take another day as their preferred holiday, no questions asked. (Manager approval was still required to ensure logistics and coverage, but no scrutiny as to the holiday itself.)

The complexity of HR operations in a multinational organization can be mind-numbing, but the program's simplicity is admirable. Work on a holiday, mark it as a Flexible Public Holiday in the HR system. Then take your preferred day off and notate it as a Flexible Public Holiday Observed in the HR system.

"But wait...how do we know someone isn't just gaming the system?"

Good question. Spotify doesn't care. They put it like this: "Well, what if they were to? It's still work one day for another off, so there is no cost involved. And we trust our employees with our entire business and future; why wouldn't we trust them with this as well? This has also not proven to be an issue."

Now, you might well be pondering all the possible exceptions to the rule, and there certainly are some, but let's stick with the basic facts here. People who feel trusted will do better work. Pick your battles, hold people accountable, and err on the side of trusting people rather than not.

And those serving your customers, they need your trust as much as anyone. Probably more.

Extending trust builds trust, and people will more often than not repay it. And be more engaged and involved in their work.

And not bitch about you on Glassdoor.

Amplified Idea

Have a trust talk. The goal? To build a high-trust environment. Here are some questions to pose to your team:

- What does it feel like to be trusted?
- What are examples in this space where you have been trusted, and what was the impact?
- What are some behaviors and symbols in your environment that tell people they are trusted? (For example, not having a formal arrival time at work or an open dress code.)
- What are symbols or behaviors that send a signal that people aren't trusted? (For example, having to document where you spend your time every moment of the day. Ugh!)

Using the responses to these questions, begin to discuss trust as a process, a journey, but one that requires actionable behaviors everyone can implement to reach the goal. What will you measure to guarantee that you are on the right path? Before ending the meeting, have each person identify one specific opportunity, on top of what you do now, to extend trust, enable, and empower.

A small change can make a huge difference. Extensions of empowerment, coupled with autonomous decision-making, can lead to deeper engagement and company or brand loyalty. And that goes for even the highest-end brands.

Puttin' on the Ritz.
The Ritz-Carlton, that is.

High-end luxury comes with equivalent expectations. Customers pay top dollar to stay at Ritz-Carlton properties and demand not only luxury but impeccable customer service. And (this is true for almost all companies) their frontline employees most directly influence what kind of experience customers will have. They are the ones in close contact with the customer and most immediately in the line of fire when things go awry.

Knowing this, Ritz-Carlton eliminates bureaucratic muck and, instead, has put in place a "make it right budget," if you will, that gives *every single employee* the authority to spend up to two thousand dollars *per customer* to remedy customer dissatisfaction, problems, or issues.

"Two thousand dollars? That's way too much money!"

When you consider that the average Ritz-Carlton loyal customer has a lifetime relationship of well over a hundred thousand dollars, that is nothing. A drop in the proverbial (in this case, diamond-encrusted) bucket.

Here is another vital component: in addition to drastically influencing customer satisfaction, it has an enormous influence on the employees themselves. Imagine how it feels to make the call, solve the problem, draw upon your discretionary clout, expertise, and unquestioned authority to do a great job on the spot.

The Ritz-Carlton beautifully describes the value of that two grand:

> In fact, the average actual amount used on an incident is often much, much lower. There is much power for of all our Ladies & Gentlemen knowing that we truly trust them with an amount that large, per incident. They are able to make decisions in the moment to quickly resolve a guest issue or to make an experience beautiful and memorable (or both). And our Ladies & Gentlemen know they can do this on their own, regardless of their level, without having to go through levels of leadership for approval.

The amount matters less than you showing you trust your employees.

And that is pretty cool.

• •

Both the Ritz and Svenska demonstrate giving people the tools they need when they need them and empowering individuals to make the right decisions. They are making it *simple* for people to do their best work.

And that simplicity is invaluable in the current global business climate.

The rate of change, the pace of competition. The global landscape and all the complications that come with it. All these factors make it such that every business has to be quick to adapt.

We already mentioned that muck costs organizations 25 percent of their productive power, per the Bain study, but in terms of impacting the speed and ability to implement change quickly, these excessive layers of approval cost time *and* money. According to the *Harvard Business Review's* Bureaucracy Mass Index (BMI) report, the average time for approval for an unexpected (and out of the budget) expenditure is 20 days. That is a long time to wait to get support for something that might be vital in the moment!

(The number goes down to 13 days in a startup. That is better, but potentially still not quick enough!)

Which brings us to a difficult question: are you an unnecessary bottleneck?

Imagine.

All the people, living life in peace.

(Oooh hoo!)

It isn't hard to imagine the comfort that comes from knowing you are doing *the right work*. The work that matters.

Are you doing the right work? Where are you and your people spending your time?

Many of us commonly described as "knowledge workers" spend 80 to 85 percent of our time in meetings. The BMI we mentioned earlier estimates that more than one day a week — 28 percent of the time for the average workweek in the United States alone — is spent on those bureaucratic muck monsters. (My words.) Time better spent elsewhere.

Speaking of meetings…

Your meetings suck.

Yes, yours.

I know, I know, you've gotten great feedback. You've figured out the magic and oh-so-elusive perfect balance of agenda, strategy discussion, team building. People cancel other meetings just to attend yours, I know. I hear you.

But they still suck.

According to statistics, at least.

Steven Rogelberg, the author of *The Surprising Science of Meetings: How You Can Lead Your Team to Peak Performance*, and some of his colleagues at the University of North Carolina conducted a study that found that 65 percent of senior managers stated that meetings were keeping them from doing their work. 71 percent said meetings were ineffective and inefficient. And the time we spend in meetings also gets in the way of focus, and what Cal Newport, author of *Deep Work: Rules for Focused Success in a Distracted World*, calls "deep thinking." In Rogelberg's study, 64 percent said meetings come at the expense of that deep thinking, that need to focus, gain clarity, and enhance creativity.

Patrick Lencioni, the author of *The Five Dysfunctions of a Team: A Leadership Fable* and *Death by Meeting: A Leadership Fable...about Solving the Most Painful Problem in Business*, puts some suggestions forward for how to better structure meetings, including a portion that involves a popular round-robin segment where people go around the room and describe their work and challenges. It is a well-intended structure, but it becomes increasingly inefficient as the number of attendees grows. There you are, sitting around a table filled with 12 people. There are 10 minutes left in the meeting, and the first four people have already taken up 50! But you have something to say! And, you really didn't care about person number three's project planner that everyone has already agreed not to use.

Or maybe your meetings are great. I don't know.

Still, those things that are supposed to enable collaboration, transparency, and accountability sometimes get in the way of doing the proper work. They become muck when done incorrectly, and the challenge for all of us is to find areas where we can make headway.

(And if you find yourself fervently nodding your head in agreement here, it could be because Microsoft Teams reported that time spent in meetings one year into the pandemic *more than doubled*.)

Master meetings.

Let's start with fewer meetings and spend less time in them. It can be done!

• •

Case Study
Microsoft Japan recently experimented with some intriguing changes to how they do business. They reduced their workweek down to only four days during the summer of 2019. Amazingly, they found that productivity rose by 40 percent! By working less!

Because of their shorter workweek, they also adjusted their meetings' duration, reducing them from a standard hour to only 30 minutes.

And, they capped attendance at these meetings to no more than five people. More streamlined meeting times, fewer nonessential attendees. No more dreaded round-robins where you were last in the cue, waiting patiently for your turn when suddenly someone barks, "We only have one minute left — go!"

Another Japanese company, Disco, addressed the meeting challenges in an even more clever way. They created an internal system that *charged* people to have meetings. That's right. They put a price tag of a hundred dollars to rent a conference room for an appointment.

• •

Symbolically, is your session worth a hundred dollars? If the answer is no, send an email update.

Amplified Idea

To help you eliminate meeting muck, here is a list of valuable questions to ask and answer:

1. Is this meeting necessary?
2. What is the point of this meeting?
3. Who needs to be in this meeting?
4. Why is this meeting scheduled for an hour?

An alternative to round-robins and inflexible agenda-based meetings is to ask the question, "What problems do we need to solve today?" Getting focused around a pressing priority can help eliminate the filler content that often invades our discussions. With all the time spent in meetings, it can be maddening to attend them all without accomplishing anything. Do not walk out of a meeting without solving a problem!

Even if it takes work and healthy conflict, it is much better to resolve issues here than to have the same discussion over and over and over and over and over and...

If we have to spend time in meetings, let's make them as helpful as possible. Here are some additional strategies to consider:

- Use project planning software to create visibility around deliverables and progress rather than relying on status meetings.
- Scrutinize incoming meeting requests. Evaluate the value you gain or offer by attending versus the guilt you'd feel if you missed it.
- If someone wants to "get your insight on a few things," ask them to send a bullet-point overview of their needs in advance.
- Remember that the higher the headcount, the more it costs.
- One of the most essential elements yet a perennial challenge — start on time. Find a way to encourage the group directly — and create accountability around — the need to start and end on time.
- Designate one day a week as a "no meeting day." Stick to it.
- Adopt Jeff Bezos's "two pizza" guideline: the billionaire CEO of Amazon reportedly requires meetings be no larger than the number of people that two pizzas can feed. (He obviously hasn't met my son, Ryan.)
- At the end of each meeting, rate them. Have everyone rate the meeting effectiveness on a scale of 1-10. If the meeting isn't averaging on the high end, modify it to improve the score. If it is consistently below 5, why are you having this meeting?

Meetings can be fantastic ways to enhance trust and collaboration, to build alignment and momentum. When used correctly, they elevate and inspire, but when you have meetings for meeting's sake...muck. Time for an evaluation.

Speaking of...

Evaluate evaluations. (See what I did there?)
"Yeah…did you see the memo?"

Or, more specifically, have you ever seen the movie *Office Space*? Mike Judge's 1999 movie hilariously follows the employees of Initech, a software company filled with, let's just say, less-than-excited employees. (And one character, Milton, whose contract ended five years earlier, and he never found out!) In one meme-worthy scene, main character Peter Gibbons's boss, Bill Lumbergh, points out they have a bit of a problem: Peter failing to include the mandatory cover sheet with his TPS (Testing Procedure Specification) report. That scene spawned endless impressions of Lumbergh as he stands, coffee mug in hand, and says, "Yeaaaaah…if you could just make sure you do that from now on, that would be greeeat."

But what *Office Space* also did, in addition to becoming a cult classic, was highlight the pointless, meaningless, soul-sucking work that somehow exists in almost every workplace, albeit in varying degrees. TPS reports, which themselves are not bad when used properly, became synonymous with the idea that we do work that is often, well, bullshit. SSPRs, Program

David Graeber is familiar with this. In his book *Bullshit Jobs: A Theory*, PI— he discusses the prevalence of what some people would consider those types ANS of jobs and, more significantly, their emotional impact on people. (And the book cover is cool!)

Maybe we all don't have bullshit jobs, but we all have seen and have had to do, bullshit work.

The *Office Space* era's TPS reports have evolved slightly, and one of its current iterations is the PPP report: progress, plans, problems. Every week people are encouraged to document what they did that week and describe their next actions and challenges. At face value, the idea is inherently sturdy: let's communicate.

The dilemma begins when leaders use these reports, or any process, protocol, or procedure, for the sole purpose (or at least the impression) of having people *prove they were working* at work. Have you seen this before?

I have, and I'm sure my situation isn't an isolated event. A team I was on wasn't doing great, and one of the main reasons was an issue with a coworker. This person, simply, wasn't doing their job. (No, it wasn't me. Not that time.) It was burdensome on the team; the watercooler conversation regularly was filled with moans about people having to pick up the work this colleague wasn't doing. For whatever reason, perhaps a fear of conflict, no one addressed it directly with the person, so they went to management instead. And management, for whatever reason, decided the solution was for us to fill out a report.

Everyone. Every week. Fill out a report detailing the work we did, the hours we spent, the tasks we tackled. The result?

The individual not doing their job got quite adept at writing self-aggrandizing reports.

What work are you doing, and why? And is it, honestly, providing value? Or is it just work? I'm going to go back to your favorite conversation and mine for a moment: the world of performance reviews. This particular work tradition is often the "elephant in the room" (or, in the case of our dinosaurs, the mammoth): dreaded by everyone and valued by few.

And performance reviews are often a waste of time and money. One estimate calculates that a company with five thousand employees will spend the equivalent of 1.2 million dollars after factoring in time spent by all parties involved in the process! On a process that shows little hint of accomplishing the task it is designed for: improving performance! According to Gallup, only 14 percent of employees stated that their performance reviews inspired them to improve. The math does not add up.

And the icing on the cake: even people who wound up with good performance reviews *weren't happy with them*! Why would that be, you ask? Often, because the reviews were tied to pay, which rarely seems to map to the excellent performance report they just heard. They were rated "outstanding," yet their salary increase was, let's just say, underwhelming.

So, what can you do? Is there any hope of abandoning this megalodon of muck?

Many companies are trying. Established companies such as Adobe, Deloitte, Accenture, Microsoft, PricewaterhouseCoopers (now PwC), and Oppenheimer & Co., Inc., are all experimenting in slightly different ways, looking for a new solution. Some by getting rid of performance reviews altogether (yes, it is possible), some by replacing them with new systems, like getting rid of the once-a-year appraisal and instead implementing consistent feedback conversations.

Some of the most inspiring ideas are happening, yes, back in the tech world.

• •

Codeup is keenly aware of the challenges associated with hyper-growth and scaling fast. The company, which helps people transition into a career in technology by developing coding and data science skills, almost doubled in size in the last year alone. In light of these conditions, the company understands how clarity and accountability are crucial to its evolution and realizes the significance of development, team fit, and how these all play into the performance management space. As such, Codeup began an initiative to reinvent what their performance review process would be.

"There's this stigma associated with performance reviews," says Liz Maya, then Chief Operating Officer at Codeup. "We wanted something centered around our core values, building culture and accountability in the process without the legacy baggage of your typical performance reviews."

They implemented a framework called GPS, which stands for Grow, Perform, Succeed. The process begins when team members are onboarded: each team member is given as clear an outline as possible of role responsibilities, success measurements, and each employee is helped along the way with weekly or bi-weekly check-ins with his/her manager. In place of once-a-year performance reviews, quarterly conversations ensue wherein the employee assesses their performance against the company's core values and their individual goals. Their manager does the same, and the two compare notes during the four times (minimum) they meet for these sessions during the year.

This system takes the form of a developmental dialogue that is both a snapshot of the current situation and a forward-focused alignment on priorities. Unlike many formal review structures, this one is simple, short, and — perhaps of equal significance — focused on results *and* behaviors. It ensures that the person who shows up every day is not only a fit for their role but the organization and is consistently on the same page with team leaders. No surprises at the end of the year here! And, breaking with the standard in most organizations, they have removed a rating scale that consists of verbiages such as "outstanding" or "successful" or a rating scale of 1 to 5 that impacts pay. It creates a safer conversation by taking away that common fear.

Liz Maya states, "We aren't using this just as a measure of determining merit increases or promotions, or as a means of penalizing people. This has a more general focus on truly developing the person versus only being concerned with business outcomes. It also helps us identify when people are struggling sooner, and we can course correct and support them in their growth rather than penalizing them for having challenges."

Perhaps best of all, and music to my ears, it is simple. Codeup eschews the cumbersome and time-consuming review systems and instead utilizes a succinct document with questions such as "what makes your job hard?" A user-friendly protocol with a healthy dose of Muck-Be-Gone! (I should trademark that.)

Is this the right approach? Time will tell as Codeup is just beginning this journey and is sure to adjust as the process matures; so far, the feedback has been overwhelmingly positive. As a smaller company growing at pace, role fit is critical, and many of their employees have expressed that the GPS review model allows them to identify when an individual might not be the right person for a given role, and teams can initiate discussions without the threat of losing a job.

So, what about you? Where do your opportunities exist to simplify? Analyze the time you are spending against the value you are creating. In every case, create a mechanism where feedback is a normal, recurring, expected part of your team's structure.

Build foundations, not pyramids.
Next time you get a chance, listen to "Redemption Song" by Bob Marley.

A revered treasure, more folk than reggae, it is sung with only an acoustic guitar and Marley's voice, heavily drenched in reverb. It tells the powerful story of hope in the face of slavery. Stripped-down, rough, imperfect yet elegant, it is a classic example of music's ability to transcend with nothing more than a few ingredients (and a good dose of talent).

> Sometimes, less is more. What we don't do is as important as what we decide to do.

We've been making a case for reducing muck, but it isn't just about getting rid of things altogether; it is knowing where to focus and just how much effort to give.

Remember the firefighter approach? That manager who changes direction constantly, and who reacts to each message they hear with urgency? Everyone on the firefighter's team rolls their eyes when they head into a meeting, knowing that they will have three times more work than necessary after the meeting.

The firefighter needs to look at his or her priorities through a slightly different lens. Is *every* one urgent or essential? Or are they simply directions or suggestions? And the questions don't have to have a zero-sum — "It's either this or that" — answer. Instead, it may be time to slow down, to take a pause. Yes, the need for speed in organizations is often necessary, but when deciding where to focus your collective efforts, a good practice would be to first validate the ask before committing to action.

Understand its very nature: is this non-negotiable, or is there wiggle room? Is this request thoroughly thought through, or is it not yet fully formed? If it's the latter, a delay might serve everyone well.

Here's a phrase that might help — inspired procrastination.

Wayne Drummond taught me that phrase. Wayne, a fellow musician and executive director at the Georgia Professional Human Services Association, once hired me as a keynote speaker for their annual conference. He told me that after years of feeling like he had to make decisions on the spot, a lesson he had learned was to practice a little bit of inspired procrastination.

When possible, postpone — just a little bit. Gather more data. Resist the tyranny of the urgent and let a few days pass before acting. Wait a little longer. The things that an excited senior leader says in the moment aren't always going to result in the tasks that need immediate activation. Chill. Now and then, slow your roll. Don't do more work, do the right work.

Work less. It may seem like a strange change, but as David Bowie sang, "Ch-ch-changes/Turn and face the strange/Changes/Oh, look out, you rock and rollers." Speaking of ….

Changes.
Changes tick people off.

But not for the reasons you might expect. Sure, organizational change is challenging, and according to *Harvard Business Review*, around 70 percent of change initiatives fail or at least disappoint. You could undoubtedly scrutinize that statistic, and rightfully so, but for now, let's examine how people feel about change and what you as a leader can do about it.

I argue that people don't mind change itself; trying something new, the nature of potentially improving, if positioned correctly, can elicit a positive response. When it comes to personal transformation, most of us would gladly welcome some form of it — especially in the form of lost weight or surplus income! Change is not anathema to us all.

The case can also be made that while quick changes can be uncomfortable, and while planning is undoubtedly a benefit and always a luxury, rapid changes *can* happen when dire circumstances present themselves — the transition to working remotely in response to the COVID-19 pandemic clearly illustrates that. Was it perfect? Far from it. Was it possible? Absolutely!

I'm also empathetic to the struggle change presents. I get it. I feel it. (Sometimes I hate it!) But we underestimate people's ability to be resilient. We have been navigating change our entire lives. We did it every year as kids, each time we advanced a grade through school. New year, new teacher, new classmates, in some cases, new school. We have proven to be quite adept at such upheaval. (Note: Being resilient doesn't mean we won't bitch about it. We will.)

Okay, so, if this is true, why the resistance in organizations?

One reason, simply put: been there, done that.

People hustle. They build, produce, ship, execute, and make things happen. And sometimes, their endeavors feel erased by a change in corporate strategy, a new leader, or a market shift. All that work…seemingly, for nothing.

"We did this last year. Are we honestly doing this again?"

"We reorg'd three times in the last three years, and now we're starting over."

"Every new manager undoes what the previous one just did!"

Is that to say, as leaders, we should practice "inspired procrastination" every time a new project begins? Of course not, but consider this question: how hard should we expect our people to work when we know things are constantly changing? In other words, what's the least amount of work that produces the most considerable amount of result? Factoring in that things will, inevitably, change? How do we make sure we don't waste people's best efforts?

What is the 80 percent solution when it comes to change, especially when the workload is extreme?

| Leaders often try to build perfect pyramids, stone by stone, resulting in broken backs and blistered fingers, when a poured foundation alone will sometimes do.

In medical terms, what is the minimum effective dose? In asking and applying the appropriate prescription, we ensure that people don't unnecessarily overextend themselves building sandcastles in time for the rising tide.

In the world of content marketing, you will often hear the phrase "Done is better than perfect." You can obsess over impeccability, or you can move on to the next thing when you've arrived at "good enough."

To be clear, this idea is in no way advocating the production of subpar, shabby products or doing crappy work. It suggests that we be wise about building structurally minimal foundations while positioning ourselves on nimble ground so that people and systems can pivot more efficiently without the heartache and sacrifice when the design changes. The hardest part of change is feeling like the work we put in was lost, or worse, didn't matter. In these times of constant change, it is helpful to focus with a question.

What is good enough?

Navigate through noise.
Create clarified cohesion.

The final two steps in the music recording process are known as mixing and mastering. After the sound engineers have created a solid mix of each song for a new album, they then carefully work to create uniformity across all the tunes in relation to each other. They make sure the playback volume and feel are consistent, transforming the album into a cohesive collection rather than a bunch of jarringly disparate tracks that don't feel like they belong together.

The engineers also sometimes apply a process known as "gating," which filters out unnecessary sounds, frequencies, transients, and the unwanted hums and buzzes from distortion, amplification, or other causes. They also add subtle enhancements and focus on the sounds that make the music sound its best. They clarify.

The best leaders do the same. They flatten, purge, trust, and empower. They clarify what it takes to be successful and help their people navigate through the noise and course-correct in real-time. Ambiguity is the enemy.

Typically, the formal process for goal creation (usually tied to performance reviews) includes meeting with a manager and documenting a set of defined, hopefully, SMART goals (meaning specific, measurable, attainable, relevant, and time-bound; words vary, depending on whose version you use). Often, goals are created at the beginning of the year, but the assessment against those goals occurs at the end. The challenge? By the time the evaluation takes place, many of the original goals may no longer be relevant. Processes and work descriptions change. Projects scrapped. A previous manager may have put the procedures/goals in the system, and the current manager may not be aware of them. How, then, do you accurately rate performance against goals that aren't current?

This is where the value of more frequent, less formal touchpoints, such as the GPS work at Codeup, comes in handy again. It helps ensure that everyone's efforts are the right balance of timely and relevant while focusing on the true priorities, not distractions.

I "Hey…you got a sec?"

Maybe you don't. You are busy touching your phone: 2,176 times a day, to be exact. The remote research platform, dscout (no caps), performed a study following 94 people of diverse demographics; they tracked every interaction, every swipe and click on their phones for four and a half days.

They found that, in addition to the over two thousand distractions, 76 of which were used responding to texts, checking apps, and browsing the web, that the 94 users combined accumulated a whopping sixty thousand minutes on their phones in less than a week at work! If I did the math correctly, that means that their average user was on their phones for 2 hours out of a standard 40-hour week.

The applicable argument here is that they were getting work done during those touches; work has evolved into the mobile space, sure. And, yes, this was only one study with a small slice of humanity. And, yes, I know that you have multitasking mastered, and this doesn't apply to you at all, but... according to the data, it does. If you go back to Cal Newport's book, *Deep Work*, we are hurting ourselves with these constant distractions that make it harder to get work done.

At any given company at this moment, people are engaging, updating, sharing information, and collaborating over several different platforms: email, chat, Slack, Trello, Microsoft Teams — and by the time you read this, another platform will have taken the place of those. (Or added to the pile.) And while collaboration and communication are always useful, noise is not.

You may notice a dynamic wherein when you post or send something, there is this subtle (or not-so-subtle, depending on the team) expectation that someone will respond to your comment or query immediately. And not just at work; it is the same notion that plays out on social media and customer service channels. We expect responses *now*. Five minutes is too long.

But consider the downline implications: Someone is busy working. They hear or see a notification, either in response to one of their own requests or someone pings or "@ts" or emails them. They pause to respond. And work stops. When they get back to it, they have lost momentum. They may have lost track of where they were, what they were thinking, or even what they were working on.

Sometimes people are working but haven't checked in for a while and stop working to check if someone has reached out, and then they feel compelled to respond. Sometimes, people aren't working at all. They are just continuously active via these channels to show — stay with me here — that they are working!

Is this clear as mud yet?

What are you expecting — and subtly motivating — people to do?

Do you, as a leader, want people to be 100 percent immediately available? Or do you want them to do high-quality work even if there is a lag time in between communications? This, again, isn't a zero-sum game. Some people's job *is* to be available and respond immediately, certainly. The question remains, what are you rewarding people for doing?

The navigation.

Move people towards success.

For many workers in today's connected workforce, especially as we transition more and more to remote work, leaders are subtly — or explicitly — creating a system to incentivize certain behaviors over others. Think back to our conversation on the muck that is indiscernible infrastructure. We need to be mindful of which expectations and behaviors add to the muck and get in the way of the work that adds value. Here are some exaggerated (and hopefully fun) examples to make the point:

In a recent team meeting, your manager praised Diego for the hours he's been putting in. He's always the first one in and the last to leave. Great job, Diego!

But wait. Are we paying Diego for being present for long periods or for producing high quality work? He does a good job, but not all his daily activities relate to work. During those long hours, Diego comes in, gets coffee, shops online, talks to Chanel in accounting (they might be dating), goes to the midmorning meeting, sends several cat memes to the Slack channel (which are fantastic!), asks what people are doing for lunch, goes to lunch. After lunch, he hits the gym. (It's great that the company culture focuses on employee health, nothing wrong with that. Truthfully, he's looking great these days. Those crunches are working!) Afternoon Starbucks run, a few emails, including project updates. Next thing you know, the end of the day has come, and you pack up to leave. As you say goodbye, he says, "Is this day over already? I can't possibly leave yet. Too much on my plate. Have a great night!"

Look, I'm not dissing on Diego. Or his abs. (Bastard!) Nor am I dictating a strict "must work nonstop during these hours" mandate. I'm just using an exaggerated example to illustrate that sometimes we, as leaders, place a premium on certain activities over others, and not all of them are the ones that add value.

Hours versus impact.

Activity versus value.

Volume versus efficiency.

And then we create this "cult of the busy" where people send a ton of emails — always "available" in our communication channels — and set up numerous meetings and inviting everyone. Is this what you need your people to do?

So. Much. Noise!

Maybe you *need* people in your company to do this and, cool if that is the case. No muck to see here. But I'd posit that, for many of us, this is not what we get paid to do.

I recently had a chat with a vice president at a software as a service (SAAS) company. The CEO had just told him that he wasn't showing as "available" enough on Slack. His team used the platform as their central means of communication, and the CEO had noticed his status was more yellow and red than green. (Question here: is this where a CEO should be spending their time?) The VP pushed back; he simply didn't want to send the message that his people had to chain themselves to the Slack channel. He didn't want them to think that being immediately responsive was more important than being focused. He actively fought the "always available" culture and set a precedent for allowing people a reasonable amount of time between asking and receiving. He wanted his people locked-in on their immediate priorities and knew they would text or call him about anything important. His direct reports didn't seem to have an issue, yet the CEO felt that the perception of availability and quick responses were the priority.

Who is right?

There's another part here that we'll discuss later when we get to Authenticity, but, briefly, other messages a leader sends when they are always showing as "active" or "available," even on the weekends or days off, are:

1. they expect everyone else to be as well and
2. they are always watching what you are doing.

Are those the messages you want to send?

Amplified Idea

Formalize the expectations.

Establish group norms for what a "logical availability/minimal distraction/maximum value" workplace looks like and how you behave in it. What can you commit to? What is a reasonable timeframe for people to be unavailable or offline? Not for the sake of avoiding each other, mind you, but to give people the time, space, and focus to do the right work and to know what work it is that your organization places value on.

Ask people how they do their best work. What do they need? Some best practices include working in uninterrupted blocks, only connecting via email or chat every couple of hours. Some teams only process email twice a day, at the beginning and end of their shift. The nature of your work will dictate a lot of these parameters but find a reasonable compromise. Establish what the protocol is when things are urgent, perhaps a text when something is truly time-sensitive. Be careful, however, not to think everything is urgent. If everything is, nothing is.

This will require some work and discussion, perhaps even debate, but walking out with a shared pledge to moving forward with these agreements in place is key. Try them out for a quarter, then modify as needed.

Work can be challenging enough. The last thing you need is all that noise. All that muck.

| Effective leaders *navigate through noise* to create a focused signal, a clear path forward for those they lead.

Make small change.

Small Change. Tom Waits.

When I was first introduced to Waits's 1976 album in the mid-'90s, it changed the way I thought about — and listened to — music. Tom Waits isn't always easy to hear, or understand, for that matter. He can be a little out there. His voice (imagine crushed cigarettes and broken metal getting into a fight with the ghost of Louis Armstrong) is distinctive yet jarring when it first connects with your ears. *Small Change* is a character in one of his songs who gets killed with his own gun. Waits put it more poetically, "Small Change got rained on with his own .38."

The whole album has a nuanced simplicity in its arrangement, usually a piano, some strings in the background, an upright bass, on top of which is Tom Wait's wandering prose and gravelly voice. And it is oddly beautiful. Once you learn how to *listen* to his voice, and it does take a bit of an investment, it is suddenly like Brussel sprouts, once hated, now loved.

Why the Tom Waits reference? Small change and simplicity. Like learning to listen differently, we have an opportunity to think differently about how we can have the most significant impact on our "audience": our people. How we can make it simple for them to do their best work. In taking these steps, we increase the value they add to the organization and create an emotional connection and psychological commitment. We invite real engagement.

I'll close this section on Simplicity with two ideas.

First, what is commonly called Gall's Law. John Gall wrote in his book *Systemantics: How Systems Really Work and How They Fail* that, "A complex system that works is invariably found to have evolved from a simple system that worked."

Focusing on Simplicity is always a great place to begin.

If you are going to create and enforce a policy in your workplace, make it this one and apply it to everything — a policy of simplicity.

And, second, small changes make a big difference. We don't have to do everything; we have to do the right things.

What things are you going to change NOW?

▶ Playlist

Title	Artist	Time
The Knowledge	Janet Jackson; written by J. Jackson, T. Lewis, J. Harris (A&M, 1989).	3:53
Simplicity	Tim Curry; written by T. Curry, B. Babbitt, C. Collins (A&M, 1981).	4:18
Never Said	Liz Phair; written by L. Phair (Matador, 1993).	3:16
Good as Hell	Lizzo; written by M. Jefferson E. Frederic (Atlantic, 2016).	2:40
Ac-cent-tchu-ate The Positive	Ella Fitzgerald; written by H. Arlen and J. Mercer (Verve, 1961).	3:41
A Matter of Trust	Billy Joel; written by B. Joel (Columbia, 1986).	4:09
Bang! Bang!	Dizzy Gillespie; written by J. Cuba, J. Sabater (Limelight, 1967).	3:03
Puttin' on The Ritz	Taco; written by I. Berlin (RCA Victor, 1982).	4:41
Imagine	John Lennon; written by J. Lennon and Y. Ono (Apple, 1971).	3:08
Redemption Song	Bob Marley; written by B. Marley (Island/Tuff Gong, 1980).	3:54
Changes	David Bowie; written by D. Bowie (RCA, 1972).	3:38
Small Change	Tom Waits; written by T. Waits (Asylum, 1976).	5:07

Visit ricklozano.com/resources for the complete Acoustic Leadership playlist.

Authenticity

> *Don't hide yourself in regret*
> *Just love yourself and you're set*
> *I'm on the right track, baby*
> *I was born this way*

—S. Germanotta and F. Garibay

Can you see the real me?

Can you?

In early 1992, Eric Clapton walks out on the stage to perform as part of MTV's *Unplugged* series. He says nothing, quietly picks up his acoustic Martin guitar, and he and his band, also on acoustic instruments, begin playing "Signe." It is a departure from what the audience might have expected from the British blues-rock legend: a calypso-infused instrumental, written while he was on a boat, still reeling from the tragic death of his son, Conor, less than a year before.

He performed and recorded what wound up being one of the best-selling live albums of all time. On this album, the updated version of his mega-hit "Layla" is an altogether different arrangement, slowed down, sung an octave lower, with a laid-back swing feel, quite the difference from the frenetic urgency of the original. He casually went about showing the world that you can rock with an acoustic guitar, and the rest, as they say, is history.

Despite mixed critical reviews (Greg Kot from the *Chicago Tribune* called it a "blues album for yuppies," for example), the album resonated with a broad audience. It reinvigorated Clapton's career and introduced the world to a newer song, "Tears In Heaven," a heartfelt elegy to his deceased son.

Why did this performance and recording have such widespread success, despite less-than-stellar critical reviews?

One word.

Authenticity.

Sure, there were other reasons the album was a hit; the revamped Layla was magnificent, and Clapton's chops were still at the same virtuoso level that made him a superstar in the 60s and 70s. But at its heart, it is authentic. Real. Genuine. Exposed.

This man, a revered rock legend, sat in front of the studio audience and, rather than hiding, shared his grief in the form of three songs written for his son. In an interview that later appeared in the magazine *Guitar World*, Clapton related, "I think that with what happened to me last year — the loss of my son — my audience would have been very surprised if I didn't make some reference to it. And I wouldn't want to insult them by not sharing my grief with them in some way.... It is a healing process for me, and I think it's important to share that with people who love your music."

Why share this story in a book about leadership? Because, as I heard the legendary leadership author and thought-leader John Maxwell say onstage last year, "Leadership is about influence. And the most important thing is being trustworthy" (or something close to that).

It is hard to trust something you don't feel is authentic. According to ADP research, people are 12 times more likely to be engaged in their work if they trust their leader. That comes as no surprise. Can you have confidence in someone whom you feel is hiding something? Of course not. Perhaps some of Clapton's album's appeal was that he was putting it all out there, demonstrating vulnerability and not obscuring the fact that he was still in the process of healing.

Authenticity also relies on integrity. As a concept, integrity is often interpreted as being synonymous with honesty, but it is also about being "whole." Congruent. Clapton adeptly displayed the ability to be both one of the preeminent guitar players in rock and roll and a father with a broken heart. His audience trusted him because he was authentically *whole*.

As an Acoustic Leader, you thrive by building relationships. These relationships must include trust and authenticity. It is imperative.

| Without trust, you may get results, but you will never achieve your true potential as a leader.

> *Maybe your friends think*
> *I'm just a stranger*
> *My face you'll never see no more*

—Traditional

Oh, leader, where art thou?

It has been a while since we've seen you.

I'm probably as surprised to be writing this as you may be to read it but, leaders, we need to see you from time to time. One would assume that should go without saying, but the truth is…you've been in meetings (without us).

I know, I know. After discussing this already, you are going to start thinking that I hate meetings, I don't — when they are a good use of time. If you remember, I even suggested you have a meeting — the muck meeting at the beginning of the Simplicity section. But there are some other things you should know about the efficacy of meetings and their corresponding impact on trust and authenticity. So, hang with me for a moment.

In a *Harvard Business Review* article titled "Stop the Meeting Madness," the authors relayed their findings after surveying almost two hundred senior managers across multiple industries. The data didn't tell a great story.

From a muck standpoint, productivity was taking a hit due to all the time spent in meetings:

- 65 percent of the respondents said meetings kept them from completing their work.
- 71 percent said meetings are unproductive and inefficient.
- 64 percent said meetings come at the expense of deep thinking.

There is crucial work not getting done with all the time spent in meetings! But for our current discussion on authenticity and trust, here was, perhaps, the most tragic admission. In the Rogelberg study mentioned earlier, 62 percent of respondents said that their meetings missed — get this — the opportunity to *bring people together*.

What kind of shit is this? (Cocktail time again.)

If we can't bring people together — *while in the act of literally bringing people together* — it is time we analyze what we are doing a little further, don't you think? We have to spend time not only on business initiatives but developing genuine, authentic relationships. Not just barricading ourselves behind conference room walls.

Time is trust; to spend it is to have it.

Consider that statement.

I Time is trust; to spend it is to have it.

If you, as a leader, are never around, it is going to impact confidence. How are people supposed to trust you if they never see you? You aren't just at risk of being seeing as inauthentic. You are invisible!

And the occurrences of leadership invisibility seem to increase the further up the leadership chain one climbs, particularly in larger organizations. I remember working for a company where the senior leader in the region worked on the 53rd floor of a downtown building. The entire floor shielded him and his immediate staff from most other human contact. (Of course, it was a "him"…we'll talk about that another time.) In several years of working in this organization, I can count the number of times I saw this person, not on the one hand, but on one finger. There were emails, but many of us were left to wonder if he existed.

When I arrived in the tech world, my position reported into HR, so that's where I sat, with the HR team. The person sitting right behind me was the vice president of HR for the entire enterprise. His name is Wayne. (A different Wayne, if you are keeping track.) Years have passed, and he is now the CEO of another firm, and I work for myself and own my own company, Unlock & Amplify, but I very much remember how strange it seemed to me at the time to be sitting next to someone on the executive leadership team, out in the open amongst employees at every varied level and job function in the company. Didn't he belong on the 53rd floor?

Don't yell at me…but I liked working in an "open office" floor plan. I know, the open office layout has become something many people have grown to hate. Sure, it has its challenges, the inability to focus for one, but at its core, the intention is solid. It encourages communication and collaboration and as, in the case above (when it came to leadership visibility), the perception of accessibility. This guy was one of *us*.

Not only was Wayne sitting just a few feet away, but every leader — at all levels in this company — was sitting amongst everyone else. Not in some high-rise with a secured floor, but in a cubicle with no walls, set amongst frontline employees and midlevel leaders and, well, everyone. The CEO included. I brought him a breakfast taco and introduced myself the first day on the job. (By the way, if you're not from South Texas, breakfast tacos are…breakfast.)

I bring all this up to say that visibility and accessibility (or the perception thereof) *matter*. At this place, leaders were approachable, authentic people. You talked to them, saw them every day, saw the pictures on their desk, and occasionally went to lunch with them, even those you didn't report to. You knew their significant other's name.

Are you visible? Or are you stuck in meetings?

To my surprise, many of the leaders I talked to enjoyed the embedded, open office dynamic. I thought they would be annoyed with all the interruptions (ahem…like some newbie with a breakfast taco — hey, we all have to learn!), but for the most part, things worked. The employees understood when those leaders were unavailable, even when they were sitting right there. Everyone got along nicely.

Except for Cameron. I didn't like him.

I'm looking through you…

Cameron was rude.

Or at least he rubbed me that way. (And his name wasn't Cameron, I changed it out of respect…or was it? Is your name Cameron?) Cameron had this way of seeming curt. He was short and to the point in his communication, which may be an efficient technique when relationships mature and are firmly established, but in this case, it came off as, dare I say…disinterested? Cameron didn't "people" well and wasn't on my shortlist of leaders I trusted, liked, and considered authentic.

Until he was.

It happened instantly.

The business put something called the "Leadership Unplugged" series in place, and it was just that. A series of get-to-know-you events with leaders at all levels. Informal, casual, not recorded. Anything goes. In keeping with the themes of this book, it utilized simplicity. The only format was that the leader sat (or stood) in front of whatever audience joined that day, shared their life story, or any part they were comfortable sharing, then answered any questions.

I learned things I didn't know about Cameron and other leaders who participated, and I was surprised at the vulnerability they displayed and their willingness to put themselves out there. I learned Judy's secret to her 40-plus year marriage. (Fight like children!) I heard that Larry's family is everywhere in East Texas and Southwestern Louisiana. And I realized that Cameron hated that he came off as rude. He was aware of it. It bothered him, and he was working on it. He was painfully shy, and yet, here he was in a group of perhaps 80 people, sitting on a stool, uncomfortable as hell, and talking to us nonetheless. And he did it for an hour! Openly, transparently, just telling us who he was.

I walked out of that session, hating the fact that I had felt the way I had about him. He was a nice guy, and I hadn't given him the benefit of the doubt. (Geez...maybe I'm the rude one!) It was easier talking to him after that; I'd love to say that he got better at his "people-ing" skills. He didn't. But my perception of him did change. I understood him. I liked him. He cared about this company and the people in it. I was glad that Cameron was a leader in our company.

Amplified Idea

The Unplugged Series.

Perhaps the easiest suggestion in this entire manuscript: put in place an Unplugged series. The goal here is, as we mentioned earlier, to spend time building trust. It is an opportunity to slow down amid a rapidly evolving business climate, to have open, organic, and transparent conversations that allow people the space to get to know and understand their leaders more deeply, without the presence of a business scorecard.

People will have varying degrees of willingness to share, and that's ok. Friendliness, safety, and informality should set the tone and from there, consider having your leaders (or team members) tell their story – whatever version of it they prefer.

Some prompts that can help break the ice:

Tell us about your upbringing. Where are you from, and what was your family situation?

What was a unique or challenging thing about your youth?

What was your work journey? How did you arrive here?

What was one of your favorite jobs along the way, and why?

What do you rely on when struggles abound?

If you had a personal philosophy, what would it be?

What do you wish you could improve?

And so on. After time spent with the person sharing, open up the floor for any (appropriate) questions and celebrate the chance to slow down to build relationships. However, one rule should be put in place – and that is to demonstrate respect and attention to the person putting themselves on the spot. No phones, no texting, have everyone reschedule their calendars to be fully present, listening, interacting, and honoring the space dedicated to this person's story.

Team variation: this is also a great way to build trust in teams, and the same general framework applies. This will take more time to do it effectively, so allot ample space. One temptation is to try and do it all in one sitting and get through all the team members present. It is not impossible, but you run the risk of people's attention fading as you get to the fifth or sixth person. Consider spreading it across a few sessions with a few people sharing each time to assure consistent attention and mutual respect.

Time is trust; to spend it is to have it.

And when we are honest, visible, and transparent the trust-building process accelerates to warp speed.

...You're not the same.

As the Beatles song goes, "I'm looking through you, you're not the same." But you should be.

On stage or off.

As I'm writing this, I'm listening to the sound of Matt the Electrician singing one of my favorite songs of his called "Osaka In The Rain." Matt is the musician (yes, formerly an electrician) known as MTE, for short. He is an Austin-based singer/songwriter/folk singer and marvelous at what he does. He plays guitar, ukulele, and banjolele (as you might guess, a cross between a banjo and a ukulele), and his songs are honest, often funny, reflective, personal, some of the things I love about folk music. (Look up his songs "Got Your Back" and "For Angela/The Walmart Song," they are fantastic. Oh, but don't confuse his "For Angela" with my song from my album *Songs I Had to Get Off My Chest* — *available wherever you consume music!* My "For Angela" is about my wife and doesn't include Walmart.)

Angela and I go to his shows whenever MTE swings by Sam's Burger Joint here in town. He is masterful on stage. His fingerstyle picking technique is intricate and complicated, but Matt makes it look effortless. He talks between songs and tells you how they fit into his life, giving you the background story and characters involved. And he's accessible. You feel like you just know him when you watch him play. His concerts feel like an opportunity to catch up with an old friend.

I bring him up, though, to talk about what he does offstage. After he finishes playing every show, he heads to the back of the room near the exit doors and stands behind his merchandise table and chats with fans for almost the same amount of time he has just spent under the stage lights.

Sure, he is there to sell his CDs and T-shirts. (I always try to buy something; recall my aside about how musicians aren't making much from streaming.) But it is how he does it that makes him a great fit at this point in this conversation.

He is the same offstage as he is on it. The Matt Sever (his real name) you felt you knew when he was performing appears to be the same Matt Sever behind the table after the show. Matt is Matt, before, during, and after the show. He is patient. He talks to every single fan that wants to speak to him without rushing them along (no "Move on, people. I'm trying to sell something here!"). He is consistent and authentic.

Are you?

Which brings us to consistency.

Leaders, we have a problem.

You set the tone for company culture. If, for example, transparency is something you care about and want to cultivate in your environment (and is more than just a word on a so-called "core values" poster), then everyone should see you *behave* in ways that demonstrate transparency, not just hear you talk about it. You should be consistent.

Yet, in a study done by the Katzenbach Center, a whopping 58 percent of non-management respondents said that leaders "did not act in accordance with their words." Slight problem, you think? Hard to see leaders as authentic and trustworthy when your words and actions aren't congruent.

Our *say:do* ratio is out of balance. Is your *say:do* askew?

I had a manager (we'll call him Chuck… because his name is Chuck) who said something offhand one day that relates to this. We were walking away from lunch, and he was about to head into his fourth meeting of the day (meetings — see what I mean?) when he said, "Here we go…time to put on my 'manager hat.'"

In this case, he was only kidding, but this type of thinking is more prevalent than that seemingly innocuous comment suggests. Have you ever heard this? People feeling like they have to be **different** to lead? They have to assume manager mode. Leader mode. Not me mode. Lots of modes to keep track of, don't you think?

Consider the big picture. Consistency, trust, and authenticity indicate a balanced *say:do* ratio, that you walk the walk, talk the talk, and demonstrate the behaviors you expect of others. Consistency also means people know what to expect every day. You are the same *person* even when you are acting in a leader capacity. Anything less is inauthentic.

So, who are you? What do you need people to know about the authentic you, even when your behaviors might sway in the changing circumstantial breezes? (Ooh, that was poetic!) What are the anchors that you and your people can hold onto even when work is challenging?

Amplified Idea

Conduct a values exercise.

Not sure where to start? No problem. There are plenty on the internet!

Seriously, type the term "personal values" into the search box and peruse the lists that appear. (By the way, I prefer to search through "personal" values versus "leadership" values as they seem to allow for more personalization and resonance.)

Pick your top 10 values, the ones you consider to be the drivers of your being. Values that speak to the essence of who you are, what you believe, and where your soul resides. From that list of 10, imagine you find yourself in a mission-critical situation. Which 5 values will your team see now?

Finally, narrow it down to three — the three essential value words that describe who you genuinely are. Do they feel like a fit? Great.

Dedicate the time to discuss them with your teams. Elaborate — what do these words mean? For example, if fairness is one of your three core values, people need to know that the best way to connect with you is by demonstrating how well they take everyone on the team into consideration, how equitably things will affect all persons involved.

If responsibility is a driving value, people should know that above all else, for you, taking ownership of a situation is critical. And that sudden take-charge behavior they see coming from you is an extension of that responsibility value. Not right, nor wrong, just a default.

Ask your colleagues to come up with their values, share them. Celebrate them. Create visibility around them, be it on card stock on people's desks or via email signatures. Talk about them.

In challenging or chaotic times, people need to know how you will show up and how they can leverage these values as a language you can share, a way to connect, anchored in authentic mutual safety.

What are your three core values?

Mine are creativity, empathy, and potential with light-hearted humor as a first runner-up, which is the perfect segue to our next section.

Were you born an asshole?

Or did you work at it your whole life?

Let it be said that I received plenty of advice not to use foul language in this book. I did my best to eliminate a lot of it (yes, there was more,) but I found myself really struggling to let go of the above term for two main reasons:

1. I cuss sometimes. Not all the time, and I don't do it when I'm speaking at conferences, facilitating workshops, and certainly not when I first meet you. But outside of that, some colorful terms occasionally flow from my lips when you get to know me. Not to make excuses, but I didn't feel that I could talk about authenticity and not be myself in the process. I hope you understand. And,

2. There isn't a better term for what I'm describing here. Nothing else – annoying, toxic, challenging – comes as close to inciting the desired immediate visceral reaction as the word *asshole*. And all the synonyms online were far worse options! So, there you have it.

"Were you born an asshole? Or did you work at it your whole life?"

Those are the snarky lyrics from "I-95 The Asshole Song," written by Fred Campbell and playing through my speakers right now as performed by none other than Jimmy Buffett. Talk about authentic! Buffett has made a fortune being true to himself; never easily categorized, never really topping the Billboard charts, yet incredibly successful and always willing to have fun and let the music lead him. (And, by the way, he's a sorely underappreciated songwriter. His catalog of original work is exhaustive and diverse, way beyond the familiar margarita and steel drum-infused sounds we all know. "He Went To Paris" is a powerhouse of impressive songwriting!)

In Buffett's song "Making Music for Money," you can almost hear him telling the traditional music industry, "This is just who I am. Deal with it." And he can get away with it.

But then, there's the workplace. And the a-holes who sometimes show up there, sometimes in a leadership role. Have you seen them?

Have you *been* one?

It is vital to give a cautionary caveat here to avoid potential misuse of this concept of authenticity, congruency, and values. You may have seen the tendency — and may have heard directly from leaders — a version of their "authentic self" that ends with, "That's just who I am. Deal with it."

"Don't like it? Work somewhere else."

Let's be precise. That isn't authenticity as we are discussing it; that's being an asshole.

There isn't a better way to put it. There are books on the subject! In Robert I. Sutton's appropriately titled, *The No Asshole Rule: Building a Civilized Workplace and Surviving One That Isn't,* he discusses the impact a-holes have on ruining relationships at work. I don't mean to demean (or be the asshole in this case,) but forcing everyone else to deal with you because that's "who you are" isn't going to go very far in building trusting relationships or a healthy work culture rooted in safety.

Sharing the values you uncovered in the previous Amplified Idea can help initiate the process of finding a common language amongst your teammates and should be used as a vehicle to arrive at a respectful understanding or compromise sooner, not as a justification for being a jerk.

From individual contributors to leaders, toxic employees are the most cancerous form of muck. Their ability to make work miserable is seemingly immeasurable, and they must be dealt with. (That sounded very ominous!) We'll save an in-depth conversation on this topic for another time and another book but suffice it to say that being an asshole — or tolerating them on your teams — is a sure-fire way to erode teamwork and engagement.

Don't suffer authentic assholes.

And now, we're done saying asshole.

Lovely.

In love with the shape of you.

Authentically vulnerable.

You may have noticed two trends on the bookshelves of your favorite bookstore or in your LinkedIn feed these days. First, self-help books with expletives in the title are everywhere! (Seriously! And you think I'm bad...) And second, vulnerability and psychological safety are all the rage.

And rightfully so! These concepts are important. Amy C. Edmondson of Harvard University was one of the first to popularize these terms, Brené Brown and others have expanded the conversation, but Google embedded the concept for me.

Case Study The information behemoth launched an internal study called Project Aristotle. The name comes from Aristotle's quote, "The whole is greater than the sum of its parts," and the project was conceived to answer the question, "What makes an effective team?" Was there some magic formula to help consistently create the highest performing teams, something that could be used strategically to further the chances of team success? Google was going to find out.

One of the intriguing findings that surfaced as they began poring through the data was that it didn't matter *who* was on the team; it mattered more *how* the team worked together. They found these five qualities make a good team:

1. Psychological safety
2. Dependability
3. Structure and clarity
4. Meaning
5. Impact

We'll work up from the bottom. Impact — people want to know that their efforts are making a difference, serving a purpose. They want to feel their work matters, is valued, is relevant and significant. Meaning — this is more personal than impact. It is about what each individual finds meaningful and doesn't have to be related to the work itself. Are they getting what they crave, able to use their strengths, challenged, finding ways they can be creative? Does this place feed those values we discussed earlier? Do they get to do — and be around— what matters to them?

Let's move up the list. Structure and clarity — remember our conversation about navigating through noise in Simplicity? The same goes here. Team members want clarity around how to be successful and a structure that enables them to thrive. Dependability — read: accountability. (More on that to come.)

And at the top is psychological safety. Google came to define psychological safety as people feeling "safe to take risks and be vulnerable in front of each other."

I spoke with Trista Taylor, former Googler and now CEO of Regroup, a team development company that helps innovative companies develop thriving teams at scale. During her time at Google, she helped operationalize Project Aristotle's findings, creating internal resources and services to cultivate those qualities in Google teams further. Out of the five qualities, can you guess in which two areas teams consistently asked Trista for help?

Psychological safety and structure and clarity.

According to Trista, "One simple idea to foster psychological safety is revealing more of ourselves to our teammates. Sharing who we are — our challenges, our perspectives, our ideas — and being welcoming and compassionate about what others share." And for leaders, being authentic and vulnerable was key. Also Trista, "Having the leader role model just that — acknowledging their imperfections and revealing what they are learning — allows other people to make mistakes and learn from those mistakes."

● ●

Simplicity often relies on vulnerability. Authenticity requires it. In the chapter on Opportunity, we'll discuss how achieving our next level of potential is built on this foundation.

Are you building authentic, vulnerable, safe relationships?

It requires being…

Beyond the binary.

Monday nights, Lonelyland at the Saxon Pub in Austin, Texas.

Almost every week for more than a decade, the words "Lonelyland" would appear on the marquis of the iconic bar on South Lamar Street. If you happened to step inside and move through the crowded tables towards the front of the stage, you'd see a band setting up for its standard Monday night in-house residency. Once the group was situated (and, perhaps, a Lone Star Beer later), you'd see the lead singer enter through the stage right doors, take his seat on a chair downstage, and begin to play.

If you weren't familiar, you wouldn't know that the lead singer is Bob Schneider, an Austin-based singer/songwriter and local legend. Lonelyland is the band that plays every Monday, but everyone is there to see Bob Schneider.

And what transpires at the Saxon every time he plays isn't what you get during a Bob concert you'd see on tour. The hits the audience has memorized (and filled their music libraries lists with — check out "Peaches" and "Big Blue Sea") don't get played as frequently, and he devotes time to testing out new material, trying out new approaches, lyrics, melodies. The Monday night gig has become an intimate ritual between him and his fan base, a safe space for him to try new things, and an invitation to the audience to participate in his songwriting process.

It doesn't always work. Sometimes, the songs aren't clicking, or the melodies aren't clearly defined, but the audience embraces the process. They understand that this is work in progress and they feel privileged, in a sense, to be "behind the curtain."

And once a few of those experiments are out of the way, he gets back to rocking. It is an interesting dynamic: the fans show up because they know the caliber of musician he is, but he makes himself vulnerable in a way other artists wouldn't. He shows them the challenging parts with mutual trust and camaraderie, laughing along with them when it all falls apart.

Leaders, it can be tempting to skip that part, the moments where you don't look good. To double down, gloss over. (I mean, people are looking up to you, right? You can't let them down!) But as Bob illustrates, sometimes leadership means showing people you are human, because you are. You can be both a great musician and a student of music. You can rock and not roll. You can be influential and sometimes unsure — scared even — while demonstrating courage; these things can coexist.

You can be beyond the binary.

People trust in what they see as authentic. They know when you are hiding, they can sense integrity that isn't whole. I remember a conversation with a very well-regarded midlevel leader who confided in me that sometimes she didn't know what she was doing.

"People are asking me for advice for things I don't even do well in my life!"

I congratulated her.

"You should be proud. People trust and think highly enough of you to want to hear your thoughts." And then we talked about how we, as leaders, don't always — no, can't possibly — have all the answers. We are human, just like everyone else. No one is perfect, no one has all the answers, and if they try to come off that way, they are lying!

I remember witnessing a raw moment with a CEO once, where, in front of the whole organization, he discussed how difficult the previous year had been. He explained the hard decisions he'd had to make and admitted where a couple of them had been flat wrong.

He sat, exposed and vulnerable, not on a stage, but a simple folding chair in the middle of the rest of the company. Amid a significant downturn in the business and a general unease shared by most, he inspired people through authenticity and imperfection.

▍ Being perfect is an illusion. Being authentic is magic.

Tell it like it is.

Don't be ashamed to let your conscience/Be your guide.

Aaron Neville's voice is unmistakable. From his trademark vocal vibrato to his soaring falsettos, once you've heard the New Orleans native sing, you can't miss it.

Have you heard him "Tell It Like It Is?"

Music litters many memories from my youth, an endless soundtrack I replay in my brain then sing aloud. I was in love with music early, and one of my favorite recollections is driving down the highway, all six members of my family (parents, four children) piled in a car, singing along, everything from Patsy Cline, to the Temptations, from Queen to Aaron Neville. (And of course, Willie Nelson!)

Tell it like it is/My time is too expensive/And I'm not your little boy.

Tell it like it is. It isn't always easy to do; sometimes it is even harder to hear. When was the last time someone told it to you straight?

Leadership is influence, and you do it by being flawed, human, and moving forward. The challenge is getting accurate insight into how you are perceived and getting a baseline for your "brand." It requires self-awareness, and that can be hard.

I have had the great pleasure of working with a company called Scitrain several times in the past. They run a brilliant program that helps leaders gain insight into their skills, opportunities, blind spots, and strengths. I can't get into details as the program's success depends on confidentiality, but I will say that participants walk away from that program with a sense of self-awareness they previously haven't known, saying things like...

"I had no idea."

"That was the best feedback I ever could have heard."

"Just. Wow. I have to do something about that."

This brings us to another thing around which we have to tell like it is — accountability.

Whom do you trust? Think of someone. Maybe it is a mentor. Perhaps a family member or your oldest friend. You may not always *like* them, but you trust them. Do you know why? They predictably tell it to you straight! Sometimes you love them for it. Sometimes it is maddening, sometimes it is frustrating; it is almost always unsolicited, but you trust they will act authentically, like it or not. You might not *listen* to them, but you trust them.

Much like in the Scitrain program, you depend on feedback to first understand and then hold yourself accountable. And accountability flows in many directions; you as a leader are responsible for it, you as a leader need to be open to it. And feedback, giving and receiving, is a crucial skill in your capacity as a leader. You have to tell it like it is.

Nothing kills engagement quicker than a team that believes that one of their members isn't being held accountable. Someone is underperforming, not doing their job, doing less than everyone else, and somehow still getting away with it.

And leadership isn't doing anything about it.

At least, that could be the perception. Leaders often work behind the scenes on performance improvement plans (PIPs) that they don't (and shouldn't) share with the whole team. But disengaged workers, who sense their leadership is not being authentic will form these impressions. One way we can help mitigate — or avoid — these situations is by creating an accountability culture.

What does that mean? It means you behave in ways (and expect others to do the same) that hold each other accountable. In the right place, context, and time, all of you transparently call each other out when deadlines are missed, expectations aren't met, and muck is created. You do this all respectfully and safely, of course, but if you want to eliminate people's perception of not being held accountable, you have to start by making accountability the norm, not the exception, and you have to, yes, tell it like it is.

Do you hear that sound?

It's the sound of silence, as Paul Simon put it.

And it should disturb you.

> In a culture of accountability, authenticity, and safety, people feel comfortable raising issues to leaders and **each other**.

You should be hearing and listening to lots of ideas, including those that don't mesh with yours. People should be asking questions, potentially disagreeing, openly engaging in constructive dialogue. It may not be entirely pleasant, but it's better than the alternative.

• •

In a small study done at New York University's Stern School of Business, the researchers found that 85 percent of respondents didn't feel comfortable talking to their leaders. And 85 percent of them said that the flow of potentially critical, yet essential, feedback didn't flow well up the traditional leadership hierarchies. People didn't feel safe voicing a differing view, to their leaders.

Why? Several reasons. Some of the anticipated adverse outcomes were:

- Being labeled or viewed negatively
- Damaging relationships
- Retaliation or punishment
- Negative impact on others (worried their feedback would negatively impact a coworker)

You need to examine this. If people don't feel comfortable offering ideas or opinions, you are potentially working in a vacuum, flying blind, and not getting the best solutions or results. You need people to tell you when there are issues. How else can you know? And avoidance of all four of those potential adverse outcomes is predicated on one thing: trust.

• •

Have your people seen situations where you, as the leader, lambasted someone publicly for disagreeing? Have they observed a pattern of behavior that suggests there are consequences for voicing unpopular opinions?

That's on you, leaders. Instead of portraying nay-sayers as troublemakers, you should recognize the courage it took to speak up.

Ultimately, there has to be a structure that works in each unique environment for healthy conflict and communication. It is incumbent upon leadership to create that system and demonstrate it. There must be channels for the flow of information, good and bad, norms for how people behave towards each other while still insisting on maintaining a psychologically safe environment.

Atlassian, a company known for software like Trello and Jira, builds such a system into their colorful core values. Prominently displayed on their website and in their offices is one of those values: "Open company, no bullshit." And those aren't just words on a screen; they use them as a reminder that their employees are encouraged to tell it to each other straight and demonstrate integrity while maintaining relationships. In Atlassian's view, success as a team depends on it.

| And here's the thing that people often forget, accountability *is* simplicity.

Consider this: when someone is not being held to task accordingly, leadership included, things only get more complicated. So often, we dance around difficult conversations in an attempt to avoid drama, only to inadvertently create more. Emotions get heated, situations become tenuous, hallway conversations become more prevalent while, at the same time, actual discussion in team meetings is diminished. People either wind up taking on more because someone else isn't doing their share, or they wind up doing less because, hey! Why should they do things other people aren't doing? Not having a liability structure in place creates more work and stress, not less. It is quicker, less resource-consuming, and *simpler* to hold people accountable!

Easy? No.

Hard? Probably.

But worth it.

Set the precedent that honest and respectful accountability is the norm. If you don't, you run the risk of silence becoming the norm. In this case, silence is deafening.

Yes, the reality is often nuanced, and humans are multi-dimensional creatures, but really, accountability doesn't have to be personal; in fact, it is inherently objective. If we have created cascading clarity around what outcomes are expected and visibility around the anticipated results, holding someone accountable is not an attack; it is a neutral observation. Things either happened, or they didn't. Results were met, or they weren't. You either did what you said you were going to do, or I'm going to tell you that you didn't in a safe, respectful, yet urgent manner.

The Entrepreneurial Operation System®, or EOS, as presented in the book, *Traction,* by Gino Wickman, introduces several uncomplicated activities to create this simple accountability in team meetings. Using well-defined measurement scorecards and goals, known as Rocks in this model, team members volunteer a simple "yes/no" answer as to whether or not they met their goal. In this case, it is absolutely binary. If there is disagreement about whether or not that answer is legitimate, the discussion immediately gets noted on a list where issues are captured and discussed later in the meeting and hopefully resolved.

The same clean process is repeated in multiple areas, for example, behavioral expectations. A certain standard is set for behavioral expectations against the company's core values and, in front of each other, people are rated with one of three criteria: a "plus" if they demonstrate that core value, a "minus" if there is no observation or negative examples of that core value, or a "plus/minus" if their behavior is inconsistent. The overall scores reveal that this person is – or isn't – aligned with expectations in relation to the established standard. The person either improves behaviors or is not a match for the company or a team fit. They are encouraged to seek a better fit for their skills at another organization.

Hopefully, this happens voluntarily, with a mutual understanding and respect for the person and the situation. If not, sometimes people need to be fired. Winning teams hold people accountable.

We are the champions, my friend.
But we won't get there without accountability and communication.

Tim Duncan. David (The Admiral) Robinson. Tony Parker. Manu Ginobli. Do those names ring a bell? If you are a fan of the National Basketball Association, or the NBA, you might recognize those athletes as some of the most celebrated basketball team members of the San Antonio Spurs. My favorite team. #gospursgo

Now, I generally try to stay away from sports anecdotes as they are a bit cliché, but for our purposes, it just works. I remember attending a game once where my Spurs were playing their upstate rivals, the Dallas Mavericks. We had obtained seats very close to the floor (man, those guys are tall!) and I was a bit surprised to hear the constant chatter (expletives and all) amongst the players, staff, and coaches. You don't hear it so much watching the games on television, but close-up, it is impossible not to hear. Players are barking at each other back and forth...

"Hey, that's your guy; you missed your assignment."

"No. No. No. That's not how we do this. That's not our style."

"You're playing soft. Get in there, make some contact."

"What the hell are you doing? Stop throwing the ball away!"

Players are holding themselves accountable...

"My bad yo. That was all me."

"Nope. Not gonna miss that again. Get the ball to me."

But rebounding directly off of the sound of players chastising each other, you also hear platitudes:

"Way to move the ball!"

"This! This is what this team does. Play like that and they can't stop us!"

"That's what I'm talking about! You got this!"

"See that? You did it. I'm going to set you up like that every time because I believe in you!"

Constant communication. Pervasive accountability. Everyone focused on a shared goal. Unselfish collaboration. Role clarity. Leadership. My San Antonio Spurs went on to win the NBA championship that year. It was fascinating to watch them; they put on a clinic in true teamwork. It was the best version of that team I had ever seen.

Amplified Idea

One of the most powerful tools I utilize in my leadership team workshops is a live dialogue around creating this team's "best possible version." It takes some setup and a *very* carefully facilitated discussion, but it is invaluable. After defining the team's goals, values, strengths, and challenges, and what the "best possible version of this team" looks like, we begin the activity. In it, each team member, one by one, goes around the room and tells every other member of the team the behaviors that are helping create that "best version" and behaviors that are inhibiting, impeding, or derailing it. Each person gives both pieces of feedback and receives it.

The leader hears it first. What behaviors is she exhibiting that are helping create that next great version? What actions are getting in the way? Then on to the person to their left. It helps to give everyone advance notice, so people are emotionally prepared and have time to think through specific behavioral examples to make this as productive as possible.

The only other rule, besides professionalism and mutual respect, is that after you hear what your colleagues have to say, you respond with either a "Thank you" or a "Please give me an example so I can better understand."

If you think about the highest-performing teams, at work, in sports, in your communities, this exercise — or some version of it — is what they do. They have the difficult conversations, openly and honestly, hold each other accountable, and then get back to work trying to be the best. As a team.

Simple but powerful. Again, the leader sets the tone, but it is on everyone to keep it safe.

Speaking of tone, back to the music.

Everybody needs somebody to love.
"We're putting the band back together."

In the classic film, *The Blues Brothers*, Jake and Elwood Blues are on a mission to do just that — put the band back together. In the process, they include songs from jazz and soul icons, many of whom appear in the movie

— Cab Calloway, Ray Charles, and the awesome Aretha Franklin. The main actors, John Belushi and Dan Aykroyd, in their trademark fedora hats, black suits, and sunglasses, appear as the Blues Brothers, creating a legacy that will live on in memorabilia and memory throughout the world.

And you might not know it, but you want to be in a band.

Yes, even if you consider yourself an introvert.

According to ADP research, someone is two and a half times more likely to be fully engaged in their work if they feel like they are a part of a team. Engagement is often linked to how employees feel about their bosses, and, yes, that certainly is a factor. But this study emphasizes that performance and feelings about work are also frequently connected with colleagues and coworkers, not just our leaders.

TINYpulse, a software company that develops employee feedback tools, shared survey results showing similar themes. Their respondents indicated that their overall engagement at work was tied to coworkers 23 percent more than to leadership! Now, data and statistics should always be taken with a particular bit of measure, but teams are essential. They play a massive part in how businesses get work done, and as a leader, you are up front and center stage as the band is performing. You want to be a part of a band that rocks!

Like The Cat Empire.

Remember my earlier reference to the Australian group, The Cat Empire? (Music is the language of us all!) Their music just launched in my current playlist. (For those of you in the future reading this, Google what Spotify was. Or maybe you don't even have Google…do that thing where you tap on the implant next to your eyeball.)

The Cat Empire performs this unique mix of reggae, salsa, ska, world music — and it is extraordinary. They are a great example of going "beyond the binary"; they draw on multiple musical influences from around the world, and it all comes together. They own it, pay respect to the traditions and musicians whose styles they integrate into their sound, and proceed to pack concert venues from Melbourne to Manchester!

(You wouldn't know it, but I took a break at this point in the writing. Dancing may or may not have occurred.)

On one of their early albums, The Cat Empire does a song called "Manifesto," about just that. Who the band is, what they believe in, what values they uphold. What they stand for.

| What is your team's manifesto?

It has to start with a shared vision, of course, an idea of why we are here, what we are about, and how, as a group, we collaborate to reach success. Britt Andreatta has written several books on how brain science impacts everything from learning to teaming and suggests that you start by defining whether collaboration is even the goal. In her book, *Wired to Connect: The Brain Science of Teams and a New Model for Creating Collaboration and Inclusion*, she distinguishes between three types of teamwork: collaboration, cooperation, and coordination. Each accomplishes a different goal and requires unique skill sets. To maximize team performance, she asks us to identify which activity (and when) is suitable for our team or project; and develop the skills to move seamlessly between them as needed.

A great leader initiates that dialogue and invites team members to define their manifesto, their agreed-upon ways of working, the norms, boundaries, and expectations for how they work together.

And *everybody* holds *everybody* accountable for it.

Spotify is proud of its manifesto. They consider their whole company a band, and their declaration includes their values:

- Innovative
- Sincere
- Passionate
- Collaborative
- Playful

What about your team? It might be time to manifest a manifesto. Feel free to combine this activity with the values exercise described in one of the previous Amplified Ideas. Have fun with it. Celebrate it.

Time to get the band back together. Speaking of bands…

Joe's Bar. Colorado. Somewhere in my mid-20s.

I wound up playing Friday nights there for a while, 9 p.m. until close. The place wasn't called Joe's Bar, but we all referred to it as such. Joe was the owner and also a bass and guitar player in the group. We weren't officially a band, more a collection of people who played together, a rotating motley crew of characters with varying skill levels and questionable backgrounds.

I was usually the lead singer and guitar player, but I found myself sitting behind the drums one fateful night. (Our drummer that night left, mid-gig, without saying anything or giving anyone notice. And he didn't come back. Ever. I never saw him again.)

We took a break, and after a half-hour of waiting, we debated how to move on.

"Do you play drums, Rick?"

"Uh, not really. Do you?"

"No. Have you ever tried?"

"Well, I've messed around, but I don't know what I'm doing."

"You're hired."

So, I jumped behind the kit and did my best Charlie Watts imitation, and the show went on! I didn't know how to play drums, but that didn't matter in Joe's bar. Luckily, we were decent enough, and the patrons drank sufficiently, so it worked out just fine.

We played together on and off over a few years, with a core of three or four of us. We never practiced. We just showed up and blasted out songs we knew (and didn't), jammed through breakups, biker fights, and Jell-O wrestling. (That was…a spectacle.)

I loved it. I learned how to be a working musician, how to create a cohesive team, how to (luckily) keep myself alive in less-than-ideal circumstances. It was fun jumping on (and around) the stage. We all knew why we were there: we loved music and performing. We may not have always sounded radioworthy, but we were a good band.

Why did this ragtag group of people perform, in many cases, better than teams with much higher levels of talent? Teamwork is a choice, and not every group of people makes that choice. It requires sacrifice, role clarity, and humility. You see it play out all the time in sports and business, in life, in bands. Sometimes the supergroups can't get their act together and manage egos, despite the overflow of skill and desire.

Acoustic Leaders build great bands. They know that a team is only as good as each individual, that each person brings a different perspective and strength, and that a cohesive group requires both a shared vision and a shared language.

Multiple tools have traditionally been used to create that language: models such as DiSC, the PACE Palette, and the HR classic MBTI (Myers & Briggs). There are valid arguments for the scientific accuracy (or complete lack thereof) of all of them. But the main point of these, or any model, is to initiate a discussion. To create a shared baseline, a mutually understood framework that we *discuss* to figure out how to leverage each other to support the team's mutual goals.

Through the years, I've used all of these different tools in some capacity, and it didn't matter which one was in play; what mattered was the things people learned about each other, shared about themselves, acknowledged needing, and were willing to give to others. The efficacy of each one depended entirely upon whether or not people "opted in."

The discussion *is* the goal, and — it doesn't matter if you use a framework like Clifton StrengthsFinder, DISC, or the "Which Game of Thrones character are you?" online quiz — if people engage in dialogue, listen to each other, we gain momentum. (I'm not going to tell you which GOT character I got. All I'll say is…she dies.)

Amplified Idea

You don't need to spend money or introduce a formal framework. Consider these questions to help your team:

- Where do I do my best work?
- What motivates me?
- When/where do you get the best of me?
- When/where do you get the worst of me?
- How can my natural talents be used to help drive change?
- What do I need in times of change?

Now, discuss.

Remember, all of these team discussions are dependent on a leader setting the tone and the expectation for how people work together. And doing so safely.

Welcome to the jungle.
We've got fun and games.

And a slide and a beer fridge...

As mentioned in Simplicity, onboarding is important. Many organizations add a form of shared identity to welcome people to the company team — a moniker or a nickname: Googlers, for instance. At Eventbrite, employees are called the Britelings. At Hootsuite, they are called Owls. You'll find fun examples popping up widely these days. And a large part of company culture is built around the practice of establishing and celebrating a collective identity.

"This is who we are!"

"You belong here. You are one of us!"

"Welcome home!"

And that's great! But here is something else to add to the conversation: cultivating a shared identity can't come at the individual's expense.

In an insightful study done at the University of Pennsylvania, researchers looked at the relationship between personal and shared identities at work. The study, titled "Breaking Them in or Eliciting Their Best? Reframing Socialization around Newcomers' Authentic Self-Expression," found the following:

Socialization theory has focused on enculturating new employees such that they develop pride in their new organization and internalize its values. We draw on authenticity research to theorize that the initial stage of socialization leads to more effective employment relationships when it instead primarily encourages newcomers to express their personal identities. Initial socialization focused on personal identity (emphasizing newcomers' authentic best selves) led to greater customer satisfaction and employee retention after six months than socialization that focused on organizational identity.

Make sense? The short version (or tl; dr — a.k.a. "too long, didn't read," for those of you not fluent in social media parlance) is that people were more engaged at work through the onboarding process when the collective celebrated them for who *they* are and what *they* bring to the organization. Does this mean that there can't be Owls, Googlers, and Britelings? Of course not, but finding the balance is vital. A suggestion from that study for helping people "self-verify," is to have them share with others two pieces of information about themselves:

1. What three words best describe you as an individual?
2. What is unique about you that leads to your happiest times and best performance at work?

Simple, right? Let's create a culture where we celebrate, honor and respect the authentic individual and the collective identity. And from time to time, let's kick it old school.

Go analog, not digital.

When in doubt, go old school.

My recording studio software is littered with digital plugins that try to recreate the sounds of so-called "retro" analog gear. The catalogs of countless music retailers carry these digital replicas of analog sounds and the equipment used before digital manipulation became omnipresent in music performance and recording. Many of them come remarkably close to the original sound you might hear on a vinyl record that so many musicians and producers — and audiophiles — swear by. Let's take a moment to distinguish between analog and digital to connect this idea to the concept of authenticity.

Want to start a fight? Ask a group of music enthusiasts what sounds better, digital or vinyl. (Then leave.) Oh yes, purists will swear by their vintage collection of vinyl Led Zeppelin 78s, and with good reason — they are technically correct! Here's a quick primer in the simplest terms I can muster:

In your typical MP3 or WAV file, the process has transpired as such: the original sound, which in itself is the definition of analog, has been captured digitally as snapshots and converted to a binary code of 1's and 0's. For CD-quality sound, that typically translates into 44.1 thousand snapshots per second at an accuracy rate of 16 bits. And yes, that sounds really good.

When you crank that jam via your Bluetooth speakers, you are now converting that digital recording of an analog file back to analog, a soundwave streaming towards your earholes. You hear a "true" reproduction of what was digitally transcribed, and it might sound killer, but it is not the soundwave of what was *actually played*.

In contrast, when a live performance (analog) records to vinyl, the vinyl grooves' captured sound mirrors the music's original waveform. And absent the presence of dust and scratches, it would play back as that authentically true sound wave of what initially occurred. Make sense? (Of course, it would sound better!)

In the analog world, assuming everything works, there is no loss of data or information! The sound has integrity.

Which brings us to an important point here in our section on authenticity...mood sweaters.

That's right, mood sweaters. Hang with me.

I recently ran across a new product that describes itself like this: *"Sensoree Mood Sweater's high collar is adorned with lights that bathe the wearer in color-based biofeedback while simultaneously communicating your inner emotions to others."*

The advertisement contains a hideous-looking sweater that looks like a cross between an electric blanket and a scarf and purports to accomplish "promoting extimacy — externalizing intimacy — relaying feelings to the outside world through language of light and color."

Color me skeptical. Mood sweaters?

Okay, I'll suspend my disbelief for a second and assume such a thing works. If, through biofeedback, as the company claims, the sweater can indicate my internal emotions externally, through a color-coded system that others can interpret, well...nice. What could possibly go wrong?

Let's see. Using the corresponding color chart, if people see my mood sweater glowing a light blue, it means I'm tranquil. I'm cool with that. They know I be *chill*.

A slightly darker blue means I'm calm and focused. Okay, that's good for them to know too. I guess.

The pinkish color indicates I'm either ruffled or excited. Huh. How would I interpret that if, say, someone displayed pink after being told overtime was required? Do they like that? Or are they mentally plotting to smash my guitar?

And then there's red. I'm either nervous or...in love.

("Hi. Um...let's talk about your performance review, shall we?")

You can probably see the potential challenge here.

You are in a meeting, and your team's array of mood sweaters are flashing with yellow, an intermittent red and green, a pink, and Rudy's is a dark blue, but he is totally not chill! What is going on here? In your brain, you're singing the lyrics to The Rainbow Connection, but this is quite the colorful disconnection! I'm sweating in my mood sweater!

Look, please know this: technology is not the answer to everything!

When we try to solve these problems, build these relationships, enhance team communication, whatever the issue is...

| Don't start with technology! Start with behavior.

Don't go digital; go analog!

So often, teams decide, "We have a communication problem. Let's implement a new tech tool that we can access 24/7 on our phones that...."

No.

You aren't solving a tech problem; you are solving (and simultaneously exacerbating) a *behavior problem*. Don't start with new policies or protocols; that's muck. Begin with practice and analog conversations. Don't spend money you don't have to; instead, agree on the desired behaviors, model them, and give people the time, coaching, and space to practice and develop.

And make the implicit, explicit. Take out the guesswork. If that sounds overly simple, that's because it is. But, amazingly, we have a way of not making things simple. Did you notice how much we had to talk about in the Simplicity section? We had a lot to discuss!

In our team communication — conflict, coaching, even crafting emails — we spend so much of our time guessing, trying to piece together clues, trying to infer what we heard or saw or experienced ourselves. Save yourself some time and emotion and *talk*!

Yes, talk! For those who aren't comfortable with that, suggest a new process or vehicle instead. Agree on a protocol, a "safe word" — anything to stop filling contextual gaps in our minds with stories and, rather, deal with facts. Again: make the implicit explicit. Don't rely on mood sweaters (I know you wanted to); get rid of the guesswork.

My favorite example of making things both authentic and explicit comes from a developer and voiceover actor named Cat Lookabaugh, who shared with me her process for building genuine relationships at work. With her permission I've been telling the story of "Cat's User Guide" for years.

As I mentioned earlier, the swift rate of change is one of the challenges of working in the tech space, where Cat and I met in one of my leadership workshops. In this world, reorganizations are the norm: retooling, reteaming, people moving around and in and out of an organization are daily occurrences.

Cat knows this, and a while back, she did something incredibly creative and appropriately technical: knowing she was going to wind up moving teams frequently, and in an attempt to speed up the get-to-know-you process, she created "Cat's User Guide." In it, Cat covers everything from installation to upgrades, and she shares clear steps to achieve "maximum functionality."

Her clever approach begins in her Table of Contents, which you can see on the following page.

Table of Contents

A problem with Cat? I know how to go about addressing it; it's all right there in her user guide! Take a look:

---

4 Troubleshooting

Cat is designed to function without problems. In the unlikely event that she begins to operate erratically or out of character, the surest way to determine the root cause is to engage in one-on-one consultation. Be prepared with a clear set of symptoms of dysfunction and your own ideas of corrective action, but encourage Cat to vocalize and explore causes, effects, and opportunities to repair the malfunction. You will find her willing to take correction, especially when she helps to design the action plan to improve.

For example, if you receive feedback from a Racker that Cat's demeanor in a meeting was inappropriate, especially if this seems to be a trend, you might follow these steps:

1. Arrange a time to meet with Cat.
2. Share the circumstances of the event and the perception of the reporter.
3. Get Cat's recollection of events.
4. Explore with her what was going on at the time, why she handled things the way she did, what warning signs she could have looked for, and how she could have responded differently.
5. Help her determine necessary actions to address the actual event (if remediation is needed) and how to move past it.
6. Where possible, encourage her to determine the corrective actions herself, offering guidance if asked.

Cat will expect to set some near-term goals, which are attainable and measurable, to track progress and improvement, following a correction. Once the new behavior is fully incorporated in to her operating system, it will no longer require special focus.

This example resonates with me because it is fun and witty, but it is also oh-so-simple. Right there. "Cat's having a rough day. Turn to the troubleshooting section on page 8. Follow these instructions...." And enjoy hours of muck-less Cat time! Cat's User Guide, a great example of transparency, clarity, and authenticity.

Great leaders — and great team members — make it simple, straightforward, and authentic.

Authentically awesome.

In the words of Montell Jordan, "This is how we do it."

Authenticity + accountability = team building gold. Whether it's demonstrating vulnerability, being consistent in how you show up, or cultivating safety, healthy and productive relationships at work depend on this magic formula.

Let's recap:

- Be accessible. People prefer leaders whom they can approach, who are one of them.
- Be consistent. That doesn't mean you can't have bad days; it means people trust who is showing up each day.
- Don't be an asshole. Enough said.
- Don't tolerate assholes. A little more said, but totally warranted.
- Be vulnerable.
- Be open, transparent, and accountable. You need feedback too.
- Be in a band that rocks. (Try stage diving, just once.)
- Be analog when appropriate. It is sometimes better than digital.
- Keep it real. It's better that way.

When you combine this focus on authenticity and accountability with simplicity and the discussions we will have in the Opportunity chapter, you help elevate everyone. You create teams that communicate and develop into the next great version of themselves, and you build robust, engaging work — and leadership — cultures.

Like a great leader should.

▶ Playlist

Title	Artist	Time
Born This Way	Lady Gaga; written by S. Germanotta and F. Garibay (Streamline, 2011).	4:20
The Real Me	The Who; written by P. Townshend (RCA, 1973).	3:21
Tears in Heaven	Eric Clapton; written by E. Clapton and W. Jennings (Warner Bros., 1991).	4:32
I'm Looking Through You	The Beatles; written by Lennon–McCartney (EMI, 1965).	2:26
Osaka In the Rain	Matt the Electrician; written by M. Sever (Matt the Electrician, 2011).	3:04
For Angela	Rick Lozano; written by R. Lozano (Rick Lozano, 2020).	2:18
1-95 (The Asshole Song)	August & The Spur of the Moment Band; written by Fred Cambell (Pantera, 1983).	3:14
He Went to Paris	Jimmy Buffett; written by J. Buffett (Dunhill, 1973).	3:29
Peaches	Bob Schneider; written by B. Schneider (Kirtland, 2011).	2:34
Tell It Like It Is	Aaron Neville; written by G. Davis and L. Diamond (Par-Lo, 1966).	2:45
Manifesto	The Cat Empire; written by J. Angus (Virgin, 2003).	2:34
This Is How We Do It	Montell Jordan; written by M. Jordan, O. Pierce, R. Walters (Def Jam, 1995).	3:59

Visit ricklozano.com/resources for the complete Acoustic Leadership playlist.

Opportunity

> *So, look at me and this opportunity*
> *You're witnessing my moment, you see*
> *My big opportunity*
> *I won't waste it, I guarantee*

—S. Furler, W. Gluck, and G. Kursten

Nirvana.

"All Apologies."

There was a general formula to the way bands and artists approached playing the MTV *Unplugged* series: showcase all of your greatest hits and do it while mainly playing acoustic instruments.

Nirvana didn't do that.

Just a short time after Eric Clapton released his *Unplugged* album, Kurt Cobain, Dave Grohl, and Krist Novoselic, the trio known as Nirvana that many credit with transforming Seattle and ushering in the grunge movement, jumped onstage in New York. Cobain played an acoustic guitar but ran it through his usual effects and amplifier to dirty up the sound a bit. A slight deviation from the norm, sure, but what truly set this performance apart from others in the series was the absence of — get this — Nirvana songs! Their performance was light on original jams and instead abundant with tunes probably unfamiliar to their audience. A song by Lead Belly, an early blues pioneer, a few songs by the progressive punk band Meat Puppets, and a sublime cover of David Bowie's "The Man Who Sold the World."

It was an incredible performance, a highlight of the *Unplugged* experiment, and a bittersweet, tragic farewell from Kurt Cobain, who died by suicide the year after.

It was also a gift. The gift of opportunity.

It was an opportunity for the band to stretch and play music their way without adhering to the status quo. It was also a chance for fans to hear Nirvana in a laid-back, nuanced, and subdued manner, showcasing a side of their talent previously unseen. And it was Nirvana's opportunity to use this stage and platform to expose the world to other people's music. To elevate others.

Imagine a world with more opportunity.

Amplified Idea

Before we continue, take a moment to ponder the following questions, perhaps even write your ideas down before reading further. (Email me your answers! I'd love to hear and compile them in a list to share with other *Acoustic Leadership* readers.)

1. Who opened a door for you or helped you in your career?
2. Who was an inspiration at work?
3. How did they impact your growth or development?

There are no wrong answers to be found here; it could be anyone. You may be thinking of someone you genuinely enjoyed working with, and that's great, but dig further. Who was *valuable* to your career, or even your life? Who helped you see or think differently? Maybe they challenged you, and perhaps they helped you identify and take advantage of opportunities previously unavailable to you.

Who are you thinking of now?

Send them a thank you card.

The person you identified is an excellent example of leadership. And there is the possibility that the person you chose didn't have a manager title. This is important to recognize because, as you well know, management and leadership are not the same things.

Oprah knows this too.

I saw her speak at a conference a few years ago, and she disclosed that she is a horrible manager. Oprah Winfrey can't do it. She doesn't *want* to do it. One of the most influential people in the world, a leader who has inspired millions of people, admitted to an audience of thousands (many of whom were managers) that she hated the idea of being in a managerial role. And won't do it.

And that's okay!

Leadership and management are two different things, which is why I have purposefully tried to avoid that word throughout this book. I have limited its use to when we explicitly discuss management, as opposed to leadership. We have to develop a culture of leaders who give the gift of opportunity *and* promote a culture that recognizes leaders who don't always get considered.

Lift every voice and sing.
Till heaven and earth ring.

We need to develop and enable leaders of all types, with and without titles. There are numerous people inside your organization who aren't managers who deserve attention and growth opportunities as *leaders*. Influential personalities who often don't get invited to the leadership conversation because they don't have a corresponding managerial role or title.

This standard, in my opinion, is a colossal blind spot in a lot of HR and talent development organizations. We set aside budgets for leadership training, then only allow people with the words "manager" or "director" to attend. Those aren't the only leaders!

I've fought with at least one of my managers on this one over the years. We'd have "closed" courses for managers in our leadership development portfolio, but those classes had concepts and models that weren't only applicable to managers. Yet, those were the only people they would want to let in since "We have to create a safe space where managers can talk about the challenges they are facing as a manager. If there were non-managers in the room, they might not be comfortable speaking up."

Me: "But we are talking about a course on giving and receiving feedback. That is something everyone needs to learn how to do."

Management: "Yes, but we have to protect our managers."

I get it. Sure, some sessions should be manager-only if the learning involves super-sensitive HR considerations, such as PIPs or exit protocol. And there is always value and the need for creating a safe learning environment. But what if you craft the conversation such that everyone felt safe and individual contributors in attendance could relate to the managers' challenges? Wouldn't that be impactful? Allowing each side to hear some of the others' struggles might create new advocates and allies, rather than camps of "others" who are deemed either knight or peasant by the leadership sword.

Most leadership concepts and skills *transcend* titles and roles. Let's give more talent access to these learning opportunities.

Another excuse for excluding non-managers is often budget, resulting in a reserved portion for "leaders only." And many off-the-shelf leadership development offerings are pricey; I'll give you that. But there are countless instances where, in addition to a leadership budget, each business unit also has a bucket of development dollars for the "general population." Money that, very frequently, goes unused. (For development purposes, at least. All too often, you'll see that money being burned at the last minute on a happy hour or Top Golf outing before they lose the funds.) Why not spend that money on individual contributors for leadership development? And, fine, have closed manager classes if you must, but make time and space for leaders who are not managers to get trained too!

There are many leaders — in your business, without titles — that get ignored, such as subject matter experts (SMEs), thought leaders, individuals with large amounts of social capital. Don't you want them leading effectively? Because, guess what? They are doing it whether you like it or not!

This viewpoint intends to be inclusive, not contrarian. Your company would benefit from examining how employees — and which employees — are chosen to attend development workshops. It would also be beneficial, in my humble opinion, to recognize the value that a more inclusive approach could have, specifically to your individual contributors.

Individual contributors want to develop, just like everyone else. Allocating development resources (and money) to non-management groups makes it clear that a company is willing to invest in its workforce at all levels; that it cares about encouraging and accelerating individual contributors' growth, even if that journey does not include management.

That it values its employees.

I heard someone (I can't remember who, but they were presumably quoting the work of Edmund Husserl) refer to this as "protention." Proactive retention. People who don't feel valued, don't see opportunities to develop in place, who don't get recognized as the leaders they are, leave. Let's proactively retain them by celebrating them as leaders with responsibilities different than that of managers. And publicly acknowledge them.

Amplified Idea

Create a monthly marketing campaign highlighting the work of individual contributors who demonstrate leadership. Perhaps a "Leaders Without Titles" series illustrating how, daily, your organization benefits from leaders of all types and that everyone can lead in some way.

If your company has defined core values that align with this type of activity, make a clear connection to the ways that organic leadership fits in with your collective values. Be specific about the leadership *behavior* in place that is worthy of recognition. Challenge your population to follow the selected contributor's example and find ways to lead in place.

And remember – select contributors from outside of management roles.

Don't just talk about the fact that management and leadership are different things; that doesn't go far enough. Lots of companies speak those words yet still fall into the trap of exclusively highlighting leaders who happen to be managers.

As a bonus, when people are treated like leaders, they act like them! They step up and build confidence, they take the initiative. They can grow as leaders in other ways. Beverly Kaye — known in the people development space for books that include *Help Them Grow or Watch Them Go: Career Conversations Organizations Need and Employees Want* — stresses that the ladder isn't the only way up. Individual contributors can develop careers without a leadership title or management responsibility. And still be leaders.

We have a tremendous opportunity here.

| Let's change the mindset that equates "moving up" with managing.

We have to follow Beverly's lead and reinvent the ladder. If we do not, it will cost us talent! Too many exit interviews reveal — too late — that employees who choose to leave a company often feel that they did not have an opportunity to expand their careers. Management was the only path forward. And consider this: sometimes, the inherent value that workers bring to an organization is *diminished* when the only option is the traditional route. And, it probably goes without saying, *not everyone should be a manager!*

We, however, do not have to follow in the well-worn footsteps described above. Here's an example from back in the world of technology.

• •

Case Study

Rackspace Technology innovatively approaches this dilemma. The company reimagined what a career path could look like for their high-level technical experts who wanted to keep their skills current, act as mentors, and still be influential in moving the organization forward — without being forced into managerial roles. They created their Technical Career Track (TCT) to give Rackers (the moniker for people who work at Rackspace) the chance to hold executive-level leadership positions, without having to let their tech expertise grow stagnant. They assume senior strategy and mentor responsibilities without having to "manage."

Rather than just paying them more (which they do, but monetary compensation only goes so far if you remember our discussions about motivation), Rackspace recognizes and utilizes these people as the leaders they are, leveraging their world-class expertise and organic social capital. The TCT participants are offered new career opportunities and top-level influence without requiring them to sacrifice the work they love in exchange for the drudgery of performance reviews. (Yes, I had to get that in there.)

People can develop as leaders in ways that don't involve the ladder. Take Google, for instance. When I spoke with Trista Taylor, CEO of Regroup, she mentioned that during her time at Google, one program that was incredibly effective in helping people develop outside of a managerial role was a program known as "g2g," or "Googler to Googler."

The g2g program was a grassroots effort in which subject matter experts volunteered to teach classes in their areas of expertise, giving back to the community and helping the People Development organization scale. These passionate instructors had the chance to grow as facilitators, influencers, and teachers and find new career paths in talent and learning development. This "teaching opportunity" allowed the volunteers to share the work they loved, lead in their own way, help others develop their skills, and also provided them with possibilities for development in their own areas of excellence.

Many individual contributors would greatly appreciate the investment of time, energy, and money in a holistic career path outside the manager track. Let's help those interested unleash their talent and become the mentors and coaches our organizations would benefit from and stop fruitlessly wondering why we are losing key talent.

Should I stay or should I go? (Or the Art of the Question.)

Does anybody really know what time it is? How will I know if he really loves me?

So many questions. The world of music offers countless examples of songs that begin with a question by myriad artists from The Clash to Chicago to Whitney Houston. These timeless classics all explore the possibilities and help us search for understanding and allow introspection.

So too, did my career begin with a question. It's how I got my first training job, just by uttering the phrase, "Great question! What do you all think?"

It's a fun story: I was applying for a job as a learning and development consultant whose role was to facilitate workshops and training for a large financial services organization. I had no direct training experience other than my brief time as a high school teacher, but I figured that wouldn't cut it. Educating kids and training adults — totally different skill sets. (Not that adults don't sometimes *behave* like children!)

As part of the interview, I was asked to present a sample teach to the group I was hoping to impress. I needed help, so I spoke with a friend who had worked for a time in the learning and development field. He offered me some unorthodox coaching:

He said, "Whatever you do, don't answer their questions."

"Huh?"

"Yeah, don't answer their questions."

"Won't that piss them off?"

"No."

"That would piss me off."

"Trust me. That is the first rule of training. When anyone asks a question, validate the question, then turn it to the group."

So, I tried it. "Lenora, that is a great question, what does the group think?" He was right. I got the job.

Years later, I still understand the value of this approach. There are numerous subtleties, and it is as much an art form as it is a science, and it is, indeed, a core facilitation skill: when possible, and in the right measure, rather than answering questions directly, turn them over to the group to get the group's input and involvement. I was soon using this and many other techniques daily, and I was fortunate to have some great mentors who helped me refine my finesse with them. I am the facilitator I am today thanks to my colleagues who observed me, gave me feedback, were patient when I pushed back (and I did), and modeled effective behaviors for me. (It just occurred to me how many of these people were true leaders and yet how few held manager titles.)

So, Facilitation Skills 101: Question.

Ask. Then listen.

Michael Bungay Stanier's books, *The Coaching Habit: Say Less, Ask More, and Change the Way You Lead Forever* and *The Advice Trap: Be Humble, Stay Curious, and Change the Way You Lead Forever* have become best-sellers in the fields of leadership and coaching. He is a great writer and speaker, and his seven-question model for providing reliably consistent coaching is a great example of what leaders need to do to help people grow: Ask a (good) question, listen.

The "advice monster," as he calls it in both books, is a challenge for so many leaders. It is so easy, so tempting to tell people what to do. To give them the answer, because — hey — you know it! Look how awesome you are! This challenge is a particular pickle for those of us who have arrived in a new position because we are experts in the function we are now leading. We have plenty of good advice, why not give it? It's quicker that way. Why not just tell people what to do?

The simple answer: learning and growth are encouraged and strengthened if people are guided in such a way as to arrive at their own conclusions. Asking the right question facilitates critical thinking and problem-solving, and, from a motivational standpoint, when people derive solutions themselves, they are more likely to commit to them than if they are simply told what to do.

It was, after all, their idea!

Michael was gracious enough to share this bit of wisdom with me as well, "Even if you know what the real challenge is (and often you don't), and even if you have a brilliant idea (and often it's not as good as you think it is) …it can be the smart leadership act to ask the question and help them find their own solution."

Wise, indeed.

Liz Wiseman puts it perfectly in her book *Multipliers: How the Best Leaders Make Everyone Smarter*. She refers to leaders who exhibit this "I must tell them" behavior as "accidental diminishers." They don't mean to hamper the process, necessarily, and might not even be aware that something is amiss, but being enamored of their own intelligence, they tend to inhibit others from drawing upon their own aptitude. This habit can potentially lead to diminished talent and potential.

We can help people grow and create opportunities for themselves by asking questions and developing self-reliance. Instances will certainly crop up where people need detailed instructions on how to proceed, but a solid approach for a good leader is this:

❙ Find opportunities to help people learn how to *think*.

What questions will help you help others?
Ask, then listen.

> *You gotta learn to listen*
> *Listen to learn*
> *You gotta learn to listen*
> *Before you get burned*

—M. Bell, D. Colvin, J. Cummings, and D. Ray

Learn to listen.

One of the highlights from The Ramones' 1989 album *Brain Drain* was the rocking "Listen to Learn." The Ramones, and their pioneering punk rock sound, blistered eardrums everywhere with three-chord romps like "Blitzkrieg Bop" and "I Wanna Be Sedated," yet even they knew the importance of stopping to listen actively. They knew that asking good questions isn't enough.

(You may very well want to crank up a Ramones tune right now. It will be good for your soul.)

Did you have a good listen?

We learn so much from listening. I spent several nights in my younger days at the Catacombs Bar in Boulder, Colorado, playing at the Monday Night Blues Jam hosted by the Lionel Young Band. Many things stand out from those nights playing the blues in the wee hours on a work night, the first of which is Lionel. He played and sang the blues, of course, but he did it in a way I had never seen before: on a violin.

A blues fiddle! Who knew?

Lionel did. And he and his band (including bass player Mark Diamond — I always wondered if that was a stage name) would play the first hour before turning it over to the list of people who had signed up to play that night, which usually consisted of a few guitar players, drummers, bass players, and singers. Someone would call out a song, provide the key, tap out the tempo, and the newly constructed band would roll with it.

Sometimes it was great — other times, a little less polished. As you can imagine, folks at many different levels of expertise and experience showed up to play each night. Some were learning, and others were far more capable. A few were professionals, joining in the fun during a night off from their regular band. It was a mish-mash of talent, a group of people aligned around a shared love of music and the blues. I miss those nights.

And during that time, I voraciously consumed as many blues records and tapes as I could, hitting the library to check out records and learn about people like Blind Lemon Jefferson, T-Bone Walker. (I named one of my bands

"Brother T-Bone," having bestowed the nickname "T-Bone" on my brother, Thomas.) I adored the insane chops of Stevie Ray Vaughan, the technique and bravado of B.B. King, the smooth slide-guitar work (and killer voice) of Bonnie Raitt, and that influenced a lot of what I tried to do on the jam nights.

So I played, yes, but mostly I just listened. To Lionel, to Mark, to what they did and how they did it, I learned some valuable skills that helped me in music and life.

And one lesson in particular:

Sometimes laying back is more important than leaning in.

When the blues jams went off the rails were the nights when someone, usually a guitar player, took the stage and decided to tear into a screaming solo. For the whole song. (Or worse yet, *two* guitar players would do it—at the same time!)

But more often than not, something would happen that would put the sound back in alignment. One of the players would walk over to the showboater and whisper in his/her ear, "lay back a little." And if the stage hog listened and layed back, the music went back to sounding decent.

All of us had to learn to listen. And someone had to be the leader.

Without it, chaos ensued.

In bands, as in every team in life, listening to the talent you surround yourself with makes all the difference.

Leaders, let's learn to listen. Ask great questions, then listen. And surround yourself and your team with talent that helps everyone grow and learn.

With a little help from my friends.

You know the tune, sung by Ringo Starr, written by Paul McCartney and John Lennon. It is only one amongst many stellar examples of incredible songs in The Beatles' anthology, perhaps the most influential catalog in modern music history.

The influence the "four lads from Liverpool" had on music is profound on its own, but when combined with the wisdom, insight, and vision of the "Fifth Beatle," their record producer, Sir George Martin, it became whole-world-changing. George Martin elevated the Beatles to a new level; they would not have been the same without him.

Similarly, we are elevated — and driven down — by the talent that surrounds us.

Which brings us to another gift that a good leader can offer: the gift of exposure. Helping people see things — through and with other people — allows them to experience a greater capacity for understanding and connection. A good leader can pair the right partners; with complementary talents and even different ways of working, each can make the other better (And, sometimes, letting go of a preconceived definition of "complementary" will help. It's not always immediately apparent what might work when two talented professionals collaborate)

A recent musical example of such a partnership was Robert Plant and Alison Krauss' unexpected pairing, thanks to the visionary producer, T Bone Burnett (yet another T Bone!) Plant, the legendary rocker from Led Zeppelin. Krauss, the bluegrass singer and fiddler. Not a combo many would have thought to put together. But the partnership worked, and the music was fantastic. They went on to tour together and earned numerous accolades, including a Grammy award in the United States.

So, dear Acoustic Leader, keep an eye out for those potential partnerships that allow unlocking something incredible. And challenge old assumptions of what you think fits. You'd be surprised. The right pairing can expedite everyone's development. Partner people with opposite strengths, with complementary talents.

And re-evaluate whom you deem a "culture fit."

Leaders must build cohesive teams. From a diversity-of-thought perspective, it is important to closely examine — and re-examine — what your definition of "culture fit" is exactly.

Culture is an integral part of every organization, and when it comes to who "fits" in an organization…sometimes assumptions need to be challenged. For instance, have you ever heard a statement like this?

"He's a veteran, so he probably likes a lot of structure, being from the military and all."

What does a statement like this smack of? Unquestioned bias? Cultural assignment? Simple stereotyping? Is a label even helpful?

During my tenure in the tech world, I often heard statements similar to the one above. As well-intentioned as we were, now and then, we'd realize that the word "culture" was inadvertently or subconsciously being used to describe someone "like us." There was an unintentional (in most cases) tendency to seek the company of colleagues that looked, acted, and worked like we did. (And who were probably close to the median age, which at the time was 32 years old. By that definition, I wasn't a culture fit in this org!)

We had to take a hard look at what we wanted to accomplish and what we meant by what we were saying. What does culture mean? Authentic workplace culture is more aligned with company values. Transparency, for example. If your company claims to value that, an important question should be, "Is this person capable of acting transparently?" If the answer is yes, that is a fit to this *one* aspect of company culture. In this case, it has nothing to do with age, attire, working style, or what music people crank in their earbuds.

A recap of our opportunity discussions thus far:

- There are leaders of all kinds in your organizations. Develop all of them. The ladder isn't the only way.
- Great leaders ask questions, then shut up and listen. They take the time to learn about people's motivations, aspirations, and goals.
- Great learning happens when you partner people with complementary and diverse talent.
- Challenge the concept of so-called "culture fit."

And now, what will prove to be your leadership secret weapon….

> *What if we're all meant to do what we secretly dream?*
> *What would you ask if you knew you could have anything?*
> *Like the mighty oak sleeps in the heart of a seed*
> *Are there miracles in you and me?*
> *You know there are*

—J. Stanfield

In the heart of a seed...

...is where the mighty oak sleeps, according to Jana Stanfield's inspiring tune, "If I Were Brave."

The leaders who are the most successful at unleashing individual talent know they should do so by *focusing* people rather than trying to *fix* them.

Stop trying to fix people. Start trying to focus them.

Spotify's corporate learning and development organization is affectionately called The Greenhouse. It's a great metaphor:

- plant the seeds,
- cultivate the environment to support growth,
- add some sunshine,
- give the seeds what they need to thrive.

To paraphrase an adage (pardon me for butchering it,) when plants don't grow, we don't blame the plant; we focus on the environment.

Leader, are you nurturing the environment around your employees with the proper growth ingredients? Are you meeting people where they are?

People have an infinite capacity to learn and grow. You can get better at almost anything with enough feedback, practice, and time. But it is that last part — time. Where exactly should you spend it?

We often start with what is "wrong" with an employee — that is the obvious place, right? But this spill-over from traditional leadership competencies is what we trip and slip in. It may be time to clean up the puddles left by this archaic system.

"Understanding business acumen, that's where you scored a three out of five. We are going to spend all our time building your acumen."

"Where are the gaps? Let's fill them! Lots of opportunities there."

Heck, that's what we learned in primary school. Bring those low grades up! Focus all your time there!

But is filling the gaps the right way to develop people? You can spend insane amounts of time and other resources trying to get better — and make your employees better — at the things where you/they aren't inherently proficient. And growth will occur, sure. But the time spent to acquire those new skills might be better spent cultivating abundant and more quickly developed talents. In other words, the places that are both what you love and where you already rock!

The CliftonStrengths movement, through Gallup, supports and evangelizes this tactic. The basic premise is that we all have specific innate patterns of behavior. These patterns, collectively called "talent themes," can be leveraged to create strengths. The terms "talent themes" and "strengths" are often, incorrectly, used interchangeably, but they differ distinctly in concept: the idea is to invest in talent themes to create strengths; use natural talents (talent themes) to create foundations of excellence (strengths.)

Furthermore, understanding the bottom of the list of 34 talent themes helps as well. You can learn what weakness you need to manage and — most pertinent to the current discussion — the places you probably don't want to spend your development dollars to get the best return for your money.

I remember a close call with putting attention (and money) on the bottom of the list. Years ago, I had a manager who was genuinely interested in my development. I loved that. It was a standard point of discussion in our meetings, and he seemed earnest in his desire to help his personnel grow. And, when he saw a clear opportunity for me, he was excited.

"Rick, I've figured out your next great development chance."

"Awesome. What is it?"

"Data visualization!"

Silence. A furrowed brow. (My "thinking face.")

"I think we should get you some training and maybe a couple of certifications in data mining and data visualization! Cool, right?"

Silence. Brow arched up. (Not my thinking face).

"You don't seem excited, Rick."

One phrase rolled around in my head. I didn't say it, but I couldn't stop thinking, "Do you even know me, bro?"

(By the way, I never use the word "bro" in conversation, not that there's anything wrong with it, but in my head, it was there. Seriously. Did he even know me?)

I immediately thought of all the spreadsheets and reports. I broke out in a cold sweat. (I'm *so* not your dude, Bro!)

So, I pushed back. I thanked him for the consideration, but the truth was, that specific opportunity and those development dollars — they needed to go to someone else. That path included not one of my areas of excellence. Or a shred of my interest. Analyzing data? Have you seen my list of talent themes? Empathy, Adaptability, Positivity, Developer. Woo.

Data visualization? Yeah, that's not me.

Before we move forward, I must be careful not to misrepresent the strengths concept; let me clarify that strength/talent theme profiles don't dictate what a person *can or can't achieve*, nor what a person *is or is not capable of doing*. Again, they highlight a collection of behaviors to which a person naturally tends. Someone with my exact talent profile might be great at data visualization. (Not entirely likely, but possible.) And since humans tend to gravitate towards roles that mirror, in a sense, their strengths, someone with a profile that includes things like Analytical, Focus, Input, and Intellection would probably be very gifted in data visualization (and similar tasks) that involve attention to detail and identifying patterns. And, most importantly, they would likely *enjoy it*. At least way more than I would have. Bro.

Suffice it to say that you get a better return by investing in what is right with people, not wrong. Not only will the results be better, but people will also feel better, happier, more fulfilled, and more engaged in the process. Not all development opportunities are the same.

Put your focus, influence, AND MONEY behind the *right* learning opportunities.

Recall our simplicity discussion, about doing the right work, getting rid of the muck, and focusing on the things that matter? The same concept applies here: encouraging all development is noble but identifying the right development opportunity is better. Spending time building (and playing to) your staff's strengths will be far more effective than trying to shore up deficiencies. Mitigate weaknesses, sure, if they are getting in the way of success. But don't spend all your time there. *Manage* vulnerabilities so that they don't get in the way. *Develop* people in areas of excellence, their jet stream. Utilize their prevailing winds, the direction of their natural flow, to get them quickly to where they need — and we need them — to go.

Focus don't fix.

And, unlike those competency-based development models would have us believe, every person *doesn't have to be great at everything!*

Look at Bob Dylan — he is a less-than-stellar harmonica player and, some might say, a questionable singer, but he is one of the most influential American songwriters ever!

(For the record, I like his voice. But I play harmonica much better.)

The seeds are planted. Leaders, you can help provide the sun. Time to get back to your roots and also time to....

Unplug.

In order to amplify.

Music, like fashion, works in cycles. Things come in and out of style, disappear for a while, then come back in a slightly different format. Roots music (vague definition, I know) is also back in vogue. Some call it Americana. (Especially in America.) But bands such as Mumford & Sons from London show that it isn't limited to the U.S. Others call it folk-rock, holler and stomp. Those all mean slightly different things, and various bands worldwide do it in uniquely creative ways while getting back to the "roots" of it all. The Lumineers, The Wood Brothers, Patti Griffin, Gillian Welch, and Nathaniel Rateliff are a few examples. (The Wood Brothers are currently on heavy rotation in my feed.)

And it doesn't just apply to that particular sound of music. Take, for instance, the modern disco of Dua Lipa. The retro soul of Amy Winehouse, the captivating work of Leon Bridges. Their music harkens back to the early days of R & B, the feel of legends like the duo of Sam and Dave, Nina Simone, and the energizing Jackie Wilson. But it doesn't stay there. It honors and respects the past but is still moving forward in a contemporary fashion with plenty of acoustic, sometimes unplugged, instruments.

One of the most fun examples of going retro/unplugged is the Asylum Street Spankers. The Spankers were a crazy collection of talent — a mix of vaudeville theatrics, country blues, swing, jazz, and comedy. Over the course of almost twenty years, they showcased nearly fifty different musicians in their ever-changing lineup! They were a joy to watch, and I distinctly remember what I thought were two amazing things:

1. They highlighted *all* their talent. In an average gig, it wasn't unusual to hear six different lead singers. They shared the stage and the spotlight.

2. In their early days, they performed entirely unplugged, with no microphones or amplifiers, reminiscent of the days of carnival barking and street busking. They did reach a point where it was logistically impossible to play to the audience sizes they were attracting and still be heard, but even then, they only relied on minimal technology.

Spank on, Spankers!

Why talk about any of this? Because sometimes, getting back to basics is the best source of inspiration.

▌ Sometimes you have to unplug to resonate.

I was facilitating a workshop a few years ago for a talent acquisition team. Cody, the group leader, called me in to help his team become more cohesive and aligned. We set aside two full days for an offsite workshop, and on the morning of the first session, we all received a text message with a selfie video from Cody. "Good morning, team!" Cody was on his treadmill walking, talking directly to his team, and smoking a cigar at the same time.

Cody told everyone how excited he was to spend time with the team (and me), how proud he was of the work they'd done to this point, how important that day and the opportunity in front of us was, and how committed he was to them. He walked, smoked, sweated a little. Then he pressed send.

Why use Cody as an example? Because he exemplifies the three foundations presented in this book:

- *Simplicity*: He chose the simplest method of communication: talking. (analog!)
- *Authenticity*: He didn't care that he was sweaty in his gym clothes, attempting to be healthy and smoking a cigar at the same time; he kept it real.

- *Opportunity*: He took the chance, in a very genuine and relatable way, to pause. To speak human-to-human, the way we used to, before the world of incessant notifications via email, text, and chat

In doing so, he built trust. And he helped avoid what I like to call...

The context conundrum.

Want a great example of a context conundrum? Look no further than Comedy Central in the sketch comedy work of Key and Peele. In one hilarious skit, the geniuses that are Keegan-Michael Key and Jordan Peele show us how sometimes technology inhibits communication rather than enables it. Key, already seeming to have a bad day, texts Peele about happy hour.

"Are we on for tonight?"

Peele, happily playing video games and smoking a doobie, casually responds, "Sure, whatever."

As the exchange continues, Key, increasingly furious, believes that his buddy is taunting him. When the oblivious Peele leisurely arrives at the bar to hang out with his friend, Key shows up with a baseball bat with nails in it ready to do some damage. To Peele's head!

It's entertaining and over-the-top, but it demonstrates something we, whether we admit it or not, do all the time: in the absence of context, we tell ourselves stories that are often misguided or in absolute opposition to — as in this example — the situation at hand.

"What did he mean by that?"

"Why hasn't she responded to my text?"

"He said my report was great. What does that mean? Was that sarcasm? He's such a jerk!"

And so on.

I kid, but I also wish to gently remind us of how much time we *waste* making up answers to things we don't (and in some cases, couldn't) know, filling all those contextual gaps with stories that we conjure with the help of a (slightly overactive) imagination. How often do we find ourselves in unpleasant situations due to a missing or assumed context, inadvertently causing strife and damaging relationships, a dynamic exacerbated by the very technology designed to help us communicate?

And how many emails do you write and rewrite to get your tone "just right?" You worry for a good reason — you have limited control over how readers perceive your intention. And depending on their state of being (as in Key's case), the likelihood of misinterpretation on the other end is high. (Like Peele!)

The solution? When possible, go old school. (Analog, remember?) Talk, face to face. Or pick up your phone and actually use it as a phone! Use videoconferencing for remote situations to reintroduce at least some body language back into your communication. Steal an idea from Cody and record a video of yourself. Above all, don't waste your time. If you find yourself at a loss for the "right" words while you write or text, that in itself could be a clue that the conversation needs to take place unplugged and live.

Amplified Idea

Conquering context conundrums.

Here's something else to consider, misunderstandings are possible even in those analog conversations. From time to time, the gap isn't created by the absence of context or the (heard or implied) tone of the words spoken or texted, it is coming from assumptions about the other party's motivations. Why are they saying this? Why are they acting this way? What do they *mean* by that, and why now? What is their intent?

To help with this, I offer three magic words.

"My intent is…"

Yup. My. Intent. Is. Three simple but powerful words that can erase the question of motivation (at least on your side) because there is no guessing — you declared it! Declare your intent; there is subtle power in doing so. Remember Cameron? The leader I initially didn't care for? This was one of his strategies. He was hard to read, he came off abruptly and tone-deaf at times, and a method he used to help minimize the potential misinterpretations that had continually plagued his less-established relationships was to say those three words, "my intent is."

Try it. It works.

Note – some people prefer the word "intention" instead of "intent." Cool. You do you.

Still three magic words.

Eliminate the context conundrum.

Sometimes you have to unplug to engage. And, as we learned from Bob Marley in the simplicity discussion, less is sometimes more.

Case Study

Let's highlight an example of the benefits of unplugging in our businesses.

Boston Consulting Group is a professional services consulting firm known for helping organizations scale, innovate, and create sustainability. BCG has a long history of recruiting countless master of business administration (MBA) grads from prestigious business schools across the world and is a sought-after destination for eager would-be consultants looking to build their careers.

Interestingly, but not altogether surprisingly, BCG ended up with a sustainability problem of their own. Burnout was high. Turnover was on the rise. The newer consultants were aware of the workload in front of them when they got hired; they expected to put in long hours, and most were okay with that. And as it turned out, the hours themselves weren't necessarily the problem.

Despite numerous attempts to create a healthy work-life balance for employees, including ample vacation time and wellness initiatives, the company — with help from Harvard Business School professor Leslie

Harlow — discovered that the challenge wasn't the work itself. It was that BCG employees, simply put, were always "on." They were continuously connected, obsessively checking in — texting, calling, messaging — cutting short personal activities or interrupting family dinners and happy hours to work, work, work. Even the best plans for carving out time for themselves fell short as something was always happening with clients; they found themselves never being able to be "off work."

Here's where PTO comes in — and not the one you're thinking of. Professor Harlow and BCG realized that this 24/7-culture of accessibility, while convenient for their clients, was horrible for their consultants. With no predictability or opportunity to unplug, they could not relax and truly achieve the work-life balance they so desired, even with ample vacation time. So, they created PTO — predictability, teaming, and open communication.

It was a counterintuitive ask, especially for a talent pool of achievers hungry to move forward. The primary concept: stop working. Unplug.

No, really, stop it.

They rolled out the program, and the first step was to agree on a specific timeframe during the week where each team member would *completely stop working*. Go completely offline. No emails, no client calls, no checking text messages. No. Work. Period.

As you can imagine, the initial transition was rough for some people.

"What happens if my client calls?"

"What happens when someone else has to cover for me?"

"Won't that make me look like a slacker?"

But they worked through it. As teams began to cover for each other during those "off" times, associates scheduled their "unplugged" hours, making plans they didn't have to cancel. The experiment soon proved to be a huge success. Each associate enjoyed a respite during the average workweek: planned, coordinated, socially and corporately acceptable, and, as it turned out, much needed.

The results speak for themselves. According to BCG, they observed a 100 percent increase in team effectiveness. Yes, 100 percent, and a 35 percent increase in value delivered to clients. The teams who incorporated PTO were happier, more productive, and more engaged in their work at BCG. Teams on the PTO program were 74 percent more likely to say they were long-term BCGers than those who did not participate.

They were doing more with less!

Working fewer hours each week, PTO participants were delivering better results and gaining a much-needed personal life. Relying on teammates strengthened trust and feelings of dependability amongst team members. Knowing when they were and weren't going to be at work forced them to plan, delegate, and prioritize their duties. And, of course, identify and remove the muck.

• •

We are at an exciting point in the evolution of business. Augmented reality, machine learning, the Internet of Things, 3D printing — innovation abounds. And not all innovation is happening in technology and products; we are amid an examination of how work gets done altogether. Multiple companies and forward-thinking executives have recently acknowledged the benefits of the opportunity to focus and reprioritize and rethink the status quo. And then the COVID-19 pandemic altered the face of the planet and pulled even the most reluctant traditionalists from the sidelines directly into the fray, replete with teams trying frantically to communicate via Zoom videoconferences to identify what was truly necessary.

But it didn't take a pandemic for other companies to decide they preferred a scaled-back approach.

• •

 **Case Study** Perpetual Guardian, a New Zealand company that handles trusts, estates, and wills, implemented a four-day *optional* workweek as a trial, well before the global crisis. For two months, employees could choose

to work four regular eight-hour days instead of five while still getting paid for five days. Who wouldn't take this? Work less, get paid the same amount? (More on this in a bit.)

The trial results were so good that the company has since shifted to a full-time four-day week. Stress levels have decreased; satisfaction has increased. Before the change, 58 percent of PG employees reported that they enjoyed an "appropriate balance of their work and personal commitments." After the shift, the number was 78 percent.

We referenced Microsoft Japan previously as another example of a company deciding to switch to a four-day workweek schedule for the summer. Their data showed similar results and included some other peripheral advantages: lower printing costs, 23 percent lower electricity costs, and a 45 percent increase in work-life balance scores — all on top of a 20 percent gain in productivity.

• •

Take a moment to reconsider how, when, and where business gets done and what work you are doing. To re-examine, reprioritize, and ignite the talent around you to build great things. As the world continues to explore remote work more deeply and reimagine what the next evolution of workspaces (physical, digital, or a blend) looks like, these conversations become increasingly significant. How can you use the core concepts of simplicity, authenticity, and opportunity to build more effective leaders, teams, and companies? It is your chance to unlock new possibilities.

It is also your chance to leave.

> *You better lose yourself in the music, the moment*
> *You own it, you betta never let it go*
> *You only got one shot, do not miss your chance to blow*

—M. Mathers

Create the space...

...for others to step into.

Rick Jernigan is a smart cookie. He was a captain in the U.S. Air Force, a clinical psychologist, and has taken that expertise and transitioned it into the world of leadership and business. He co-wrote a book called *C.O.A.C.H.* with the subtitle "The Last Act of Leading Is Leaving."

I've always admired that phrase and the idea that if a leader does their job well, they should work themselves out of a job in essence (if not always in practice). They aim to develop those they lead to the point they are no longer needed, then fly away to help others.

But leaving doesn't have to be the last act; it can be one you incorporate in current work life. It is important that, in the right circumstances, you do just that: leave. Why? Two reasons:

First, so we don't enable (or exhibit) the martyr complex.

The martyr. You know the one.

That person who is too busy to take a vacation. Ever. The lone, sad soul who publicly states they need the full five days to get their work done instead of taking the option of working one less day.

Yes, friends, the martyr. Often a leader. Always a drag.

Have you ever played the martyr?

As we've discussed, leaders have a considerable influence on workplace culture and regulating the logistics of the workflow. People are looking to you and emulating the behaviors you demonstrate whether or not you know it. And, as a society, we've seen the celebration of the cult of busy. Are you the person who wears the badge of honor for staying the longest, working the hardest, suffering the most? Are you the manager who glories in the misplaced pride of leaving earned vacation time on the table simply because "I was too busy; I had no choice?"

Moving from coffee talk to cocktail talk for a moment here, leaders — **cut that shit out**.

What is the value of setting a bad example? Of implying that people can only be successful by sacrificing their lives? Of whispering (or saying loudly) those snide comments when other people come back from vacation, "Must be nice. Wish I could take time off."?

Stop it. Just stop it. Or stop whoever is doing that at your company. Make sure leadership is setting a good example by demonstrating efficiency. Emphasize value over martyrdom, impact over hours. Show people what muck reduction looks like by doing it yourself!

Leader, if you can't ever take time off, *you are doing it wrong.*

And, secondly, if you are always around, when do others get a chance to lead? It comes down to this; sometimes your team needs you…

…to leave.

Go away. We got this.

> Your role is to help people succeed, develop career skills, facilitate self-reliance, and create opportunities for others.

Sometimes, to do that, you have to leave.

Think about it: if adults did *everything* for children, would they ever learn? That's why every young adult adventure starts with getting the parents out of the way. Leaders often need to do the same for team learning to occur. This doesn't mean you abdicate responsibility and hang your people out to dry; it means that when the situation is right, you get out of the way! Create the space that others can step into.

Here's another, more personal example: years ago, the company I was with was in the midst of its third international acquisition in the span of two short years, resulting in turmoil, confusion, a dip in employee engagement, and an increase in attrition. As our team was deployed to help devise critical go-to-market transition solutions for the company, there was a general unease about the new company strategy and a sense of loss as the company we loved changed in disconcerting ways.

Since most of the company wasn't aware of the merger, we signed nondisclosure agreements and those of us "in the know" hit the ground running. Our leader, Theresa, advised us that the task in front of us was the most critical work our team was going to do all year. The business was looking to us as leaders to do this right. This was our chance to show them what we could do.

And Theresa (her real name) had vacation time scheduled during this same period.

You've seen this play out as many times as I have: leaders cancel their vacations, infuriate their family members, lose deposit money, change plans, miss family milestones, and "happily" return to work because, damnit, that's what leaders do! Part of the job — suck it up, buttercup!

Not Theresa. Theresa went on vacation.

The following two weeks were taxing, to say the least. Working well past midnight, multiple days in a row, the team and I tried to piece together our deliverables under the most chaotic of conditions. Our stakeholders weren't sure how to help us. Our SMEs didn't know enough about the go-forward plan to be of any use. There were far too many people involved, most without a clear idea of their specific responsibility, and what, precisely, were we supposed to be delivering in the first place?

No word from Theresa.

We kept going. We put together trial versions of our projects, got scrappy with our ways of working, got creative in our approach, focused on execution rather than perfection, and got things done. We made decisions in the moment; without approval or authorization; we took ownership of what we could. And we delivered.

At last, my team had finished. On a Wednesday at noon, I notified my immediate teammates (most of whom were not involved in this project but knew something urgent was taking place as I had been pulled off of everything else) that I was going home to sleep. For the rest of the week.

Mission accomplished, adios. I didn't come back until Monday.

When I did return, Theresa was there. First, we caught up about her time off. How was the family time? Long overdue, so needed. She told me about the places they had gone and recommended a few restaurants.

Then she told me the business' reaction to the work my project team had done. "Stellar. Fantastic. People are impressed with the way you guys took charge, stepped up, and got it done." She told me about the difference made by one of my project teammates. She had assumed the leadership role: decisive, commanding, and well out of the comfort zone of her usually reserved nature. She rocked. Theresa said. "I'm so glad she's getting the recognition she deserves."

Finally, she told me how tempted she was every day to check in, to call, to cancel her vacation, to offer resources, and get involved. "But I wanted y'all to know that I trusted you to get it done." She thanked me for my work, and I thanked her for her leadership. We agreed that beer was in order and that we'd catch up later. As she walked away, she said: "I tell you what. This has been a rough year. And that — being on vacation during this whole thing — that was surprisingly the hardest thing I've had to do as a leader this entire year."

I smiled. In many ways, it was also the best thing she did as a leader that year. In retrospect, even had the entire project collapsed, it would have been a great learning experience. Thank you, Theresa, for elevating us by extracting yourself.

The gift that Hambone gave.
"Rollin' And Tumblin'."

Eric Clapton's *Unplugged* show ends with him tearing it up with a bottleneck slide on a resonator guitar, playing that barnstormer of a song. When it's over, he stands, says thank you, acknowledges his band, and leaves. And the record went on to make live recording sales history.

"Rollin' And Tumblin'" was first recorded by a gentleman named Hambone Willie Newborn. He was a relatively obscure artist who is only known to have recorded six songs, all in one recording session in 1929.

Countless versions and variations of his recording of "Rollin' And Tumblin'" live on through the works of Muddy Waters, Eric Clapton, and dozens of others. He, of course, never knew the impact he would have on others. He was, as they say, before his time. The gift that Hambone gave became an opportunity for others to shine.

The same is true for the leaders that give people the gift of opportunity. You may not know how your influence changes people's lives, and you don't do it for the recognition or acclaim; you do it from a place of service and integrity and know you have done your job when others grow.

Rock on, Hambone.

▶ Playlist

Title	Artist	Time
Opportunity	Sia; written by S. Furler, W. Gluck, and G. Kursten (RCA, 2014).	3:14
Man Who Sold The World	Nirvana; written by D. Bowie (Sony, 1993).	4:21
Learn To Listen	The Ramones; written by M. Bell, D. Colvin, J. Cummings, and D. Ray (Sire, 1989).	1:51
With A Little Help from My Friends	The Beatles; written by Lennon–McCartney (Parlopone, 1967).	2:44
Gone, Gone, Gone (Done Moved On)	Robert Plant and Allison Krauss; written by D. Everly and P. Everly (Warner Bros., 1964).	3:33
If I Were Brave	Jana Stanfield; written by J. Stanfield and J. Scott (Jana Stan Tunes, 1998).	5:02
Keep Me Around	The Wood Brothers; written by J. Rix, C. Wood, and O. Wood (Southern Ground, 2013).	3:39
Funny Cigarette	The Asylum Street Spankers; written by P. Bayless (Yellow Dog, 1996).	3:17
Lose Yourself	Eminem; written by M. Mathers (Aftermath, 2002).	5:21
Rollin' and Tumblin'	RL Burnside; traditional (Okey, 1929).	3:50

Visit ricklozano.com/resources for the complete Acoustic Leadership playlist.

The Impact

> *I think music is an instrument.*
> *It can create the initial thought patterns*
> *that can change the thinking of the people.*

—John Coltrane

Resonate.

A Martin D-15 acoustic guitar. Mahogany wood.

It's cracked and reglued in several places. The circular design around the sound-hole is missing a section from years of guitar picks repeatedly slammed into it while strumming. Though nowhere near as damaged as Willie Nelson's famous guitar, Trigger, it is still adorned with dents and nicks all over the body, having seen its share of bang-ups. It has marks that won't wipe off; between the beer, the blood, and who-knows-what-else, I've given up trying to make it look pretty.

It's my baby.

I thought for sure it was dead a couple of years ago. I was practicing a keynote, with my guitar slung over my back, as usual, when my strap broke. I've dropped this guitar countless times, but this time I knew it was bad: I heard the crack and instantly thought, "Oh, crap!" Sure enough: a six-inch-long section of the back — gone.

Somehow, the luthier geniuses at my local acoustic guitar shop, Guitar Tex, fixed it. They brought my baby back from guitar zombie land. (By the way, support small, local, independent guitar stores!) The tone has changed slightly, but the instrument still reverberates and resonates the way it should. It makes me happy, and I hope that my guitar and I have made someone smile along the way.

Just like the luthier, we can rely on resonance as one of those clues that will tell us that we're on the right track, whether we are talking about guitars or people. That's why we're here right now, talking about practicing Acoustic Leadership and developing a leadership culture that *resonates*.

If you research the definition of the term *resonate*, you will find:

- Produce or be filled with a deep reverberating sound
- To have particular meaning or importance to someone
- To affect or appeal to someone in a personal or emotional way

The second and third definitions jump out at me. Meaning. Emotion.

Remember, information without emotion means nothing. If you think about what leadership is and what it can do, that word — *resonates* — is one to embrace as our goal. It makes sense, means something, it evokes emotion and positively moves us.

It unites people.

Moreover, resonant leadership moves outward, just as analog sound waves move through the mahogany in the interior of my Martin D-15 to anyone within earshot. It inspires.

The world needs leadership now, more than ever — leaders who give people the opportunity to step into their greatness.

Leadership that resonates.

At this point, I am reminded of something known as the Pygmalion effect, the phenomenon wherein one person's expectations of another impact the other person's performance. Plainly put, when we set the bar higher for someone, their output is potentially greater. When we lower the bar based on the assumption that they can't achieve it in the first place, guess what? That's the level to which they ascend. It is a self-fulfilling prophesy where we (and others, as it turns out) create the reality we expect. If we want to develop a leadership culture, we have to raise that bar and give people the opportunity to be – and be recognized as – leaders.

What is one way that leaders can raise the bar? By tapping into the inherent power of passion and the drive for creation.

The time for creative connection.

And inspired innovation.

As demonstrated by Google's Project Aristotle, you need to create meaning, to connect people to their work. And that can be a challenge, but it is so worthwhile.

The *Harvard Business Review* states that we dedicate 40 percent of our time at work to things that give us little sense of accomplishment. It probably goes without saying...that sucks! Making work matter, making people feel connected and part of a greater whole, is essential. Often, that meaning exists at the intersection of passion, curiosity, and natural talent. Leaders help people find that place by giving them the space to create.

Sometimes it only takes 20 percent of their time.

• •

Case Study

Twenty percent time.

I remember being immediately struck by the concept when I first heard of it: encourage people to spend 20 percent of their time working on passion projects. Create something. Have fun. Do it while working. By allowing this type of work, people are intrinsically motivated to do work that matters to them and often helps the company.

3M, the company that brought you Post-It-Notes, is often credited with the first version of the notion (theirs was only 15 percent,) but Google is most often thought of in relation to it these days. In his book *Brain Rules: 12 Principles for Surviving and Thriving at Work, Home, and School,* John Medina talks about the Google culture and 20 percent time and that the allowance of creative stints that were spent on passion projects led to almost *half* of all their new products!

Atlassian also implemented a version that they call "Ship It Days." Each quarter, in true tech hackathon-style, people are given 24 hours (from Thursday overnight into Friday) to create something and "ship it." People bring innovative ideas they think can help the company; they work in a fun manner with requisite coffee and Irish whiskey, and then on Friday, they present their (slightly hungover) solutions.

The idea of igniting creativity, talent, and passion resonates on many fronts (obviously, right?). Workers appreciate the opportunity to contribute, have fun, and the companies benefit from many of the solutions. A great example of this, one that millions of people currently benefit from every day: Google used one of its 20 percent-time projects to add accessibility information into Google Maps. Way cool! Do the right thing and engage talent at the same time; everyone wins.

You can almost make the case that NOT implementing 20-percent-time would be a gross underutilization of company talent and ideas.

Goldman Sachs takes this concept to another level entirely; interesting, considering that the 150-year-old investment bank isn't exactly the first name that you'd associate with startups and innovation. Still, their GS Accelerate program is, in fact, uniquely remarkable in that it not only lets people work on passion projects but also gives them resources and funding to start their own business doing it.

Entrepreneurs pitch their ideas through several rounds of competition, and the winners are awarded two years off their regular duties — paid — and with access to all the company's resources to build the startup from scratch. Since 2018, 13 of the more than 1,500 submissions have been awarded funding. And ideas that aren't accepted are still considered for funding outside of the program.

These ideas speak to the possibilities created when your culture practices Acoustic Leadership.

When you tap into people's natural genius, unleash their potential, give them a sense of ownership, empowerment, and support, work becomes art.

Even when things don't work.

Failure as fuel.
To power the progress.

I first heard of a Fail Jam at a conference. I was on the program advisory committee for the ATD TechKnowledge conference, surrounded by intelligent, talented people. This particular event focuses on the intersection of learning and technology and is attended mainly by companies, innovators, instructional designers, and people who work to integrate technology and education.

Becca Wilson was the chairperson for the committee that year. She's a whip-smart product manager at Amazon, and she facilitated an "alternative programming" session for the conference called "Fail Jam."

The premise was simple: Share your failures. What did you do, what did you learn? How did the face-plants happen, and what were the lessons? It was intriguing to watch, hear, and be a part of the things people shared. Some were a matter of fact; others were profound, vulnerable admissions of failure — and guilt. It was fascinating — and oddly uniting — to listen to a group of strangers at a conference, taking turns standing in front of the room, talking about all the things they had screwed up. I think I speak for each person in the audience when I say that we learned through/from each speaker's failures. It was cathartic. And, as leaders do, Becca went first.

NixonMcInnes, a small social media consultancy in the UK, also instituted this practice every month while the company was in business. Their "Church of Fail" began with the phrase, "Dearly beloved, we gather here today to confess and celebrate the failures of ourselves and our colleagues." As many startups do, the company ultimately retired its brand and evolved into multiple different companies, but its practice of openness and transparency is still a great model.

In both Fail Jam and the Church of Fail, the speakers are given rousing heaps of applause — they are celebrated, in fact — for screwing up. And they are thanked for their contributions. And encouraged to fail on. They smile, commune, press forward.

Today's — and one could argue history's (hello Abraham Lincoln) — most effective leaders realize the benefits of learning through loss and failing and plowing forward. Visionaries (read: repeat failers) create an environment where they and those around them are encouraged to try new (and sometimes crazy) ideas, to help them find their purpose, their signature sound. Even when things don't work out.

Fail on, my friends!

And now, time to innovate.

More mood sweaters?

Nope, sorry.

Just more awesome examples of leaders and organizations finding new ways of working that resonate.

According to McKinsey & Company, 70 percent of senior executives view innovation as one of the top three critical drivers for their organization. But creating sustainable change at scale isn't easy! And these same leaders know that technology, while often a progressive tool for driving innovation, isn't where the magic is. 94 percent stated that *people* and corporate *culture* were the drivers of that innovation.

Here's a discouraging counter-stat: while executives emphasized the importance of innovation, the people doing the work weren't quite as enthusiastic. The previously referenced BMI Index study found that 80 percent of workers felt that their new ideas — innovative and could help the company move forward — would encounter resistance.

Muck.

How are you currently creating the conditions for innovation? Have you built in the aforementioned psychological safety, culture of trust, and forward-motion failure required? Are you letting your teams tap into their natural talents to create things that inspire?

It is important to note that innovations don't have to be life-changing or technologically advanced to impact employees and customers. Here's an example from the world of planes, trains, and automobiles: The Southern Rail in London. A train driver named Steve Copley created an innovative approach to change passengers' daily commute experiences. Using Twitter and his natural knack for humor (or humour, as they spell it there), he invented something called "Time Tunnel Train," a trivia game played while passengers rode the rail. Steve asked questions via the intercom; passengers responded via Twitter. Simple. And Time Tunnel Train was a hit; people loved the experience. Some fans even asked Southern Rail to give Copley a raise! I don't know if they did, but he did win the driver of the year award. (Good on you, Steve.)

Now, I wasn't there, and I don't have inside information about how this played out with Steve's leaders. Was there resistance? Probably. "That will annoy passengers!" was my first thought too. And maybe it did, but those that didn't want to be part of the experience pulled their noise-canceling headphones down tight and minded their own gap(s). (Get it? "Mind the gap." Sorry, I just had to. Let's move on.)

Ultimately someone had to decide: is this good for Southern Rail and the passengers on the Time Tunnel Train? Someone eventually told Steve: "Go for it. Try it out. We trust you."

And they got out of the way. And Steve and Time Tunnel Train became a hit.

Innovation depends on ideas, lots of them. Crazy ideas included. In the book, *The Medici Effect: What Elephants and Epidemics Can Teach Us about Innovation*, Frans Johansson encourages "an explosion of ideas" as the solution. He describes the process many famous inventors use to come up with their patents or inventions. A large part of the process requires focus on the number of ideas over quality: get them all out there, and it is a mathematical certainty that, sooner or later, the right solution will pop up.

Why, then, do we so often hear individual contributors complaining that managers aren't listening to their ideas? We could probably return to the muck mentality and the misaligned motivators discussion, but let's also acknowledge that we are dealing with other (mostly) human beings, and — being a manager is hard! There is a lot to think through.

So, how do we help the situation? Three words:

▌ Slow. Your. No.

That's right, slow your "no" response. Pause, resist your automatic instinct to dismiss, to move on quickly to the next topic and, instead of a "no," ask a question. Practice inspired procrastination by inviting them to elaborate.

"Tell me more."

"How does this work?"

"Help me understand…"

Even if the result doesn't adopt their idea, the talent around you is more likely to react positively to the situation if they feel that they were *heard*, and their idea was considered.

But, taking a cue from Steve Copley and realizing that communication is a two-way street (or rail in this analogy), let's help both parties find the most impactful means to engage in dialogue. What this means is that we have an opportunity to help people *be heard!*

Invest in training opportunities to help enrich communication, build skills to *present* their ideas effectively, become more adept at making their case. We all stand to benefit by refining our approach to be delivered more like this: "Here is an idea that can greatly enhance the customer experience and costs us nothing."

That sound? Music to our ears.

Improvise and adapt.

Jazz and the legendary John Coltrane.

Considered by some to be the most influential saxophonist ever to play, Coltrane's ability to connect melodies and his savant understanding of musical theory created some of the most innovative jazz (or any music) of all time. Listening to his remarkable talent on the tune "Dear Lord" hits me in the soul each time I hear it!

And, if you know anything about jazz, you know that while it requires a basic structure, most of it is improvised. Standard jazz structures start with a melody, a root phrase that defines the tune, sets the song's necessary parameters, and, from there, jazz musicians fly free. They explore every possible idea, obvious or unimaginable. They leverage their virtuosity to innovate in the musical space.

The answers are out there. Here is the structure. These are the guardrails. Go. (And sometimes break the guardrails.)

Great leaders in business and jazz are adept at enabling something I call informed improvisation. They employ the right band members, focus them on their natural abilities and strengths, and create a safe-to-fail environment, ensuring people are set up for success. Then, they stand back and let people jam.

Are you making it simple for people to do their best work? Are you encouraging or stifling innovation? When trust is in place, you give people a better opportunity to develop into their potential.

"Okay, Rick. You talk a lot about giving people autonomy and freedom, but what if they screw up?"

Good question.

But that's not the right question.

The right question is, "What kind of company are we going to *be* when they screw up?"

Hopefully, the answer is "A safe one."

Look, I'm a realist. I work in the same reality that you do, and I realize that you can't always just let people do anything and everything they want with no rules. But when we set up too many rules and become overly involved, a toxic micromanagement environment usually arises. On the flip side, I am fully aware that ineffective leadership is sometimes demonstrated by *undermanaging*! So, we must make informed decisions about when, how, and with whom we lead and know that every circumstance — and task — will likely require a unique approach and that safety (in all its forms) is paramount.

Remember that overreliance on directive behaviors we talked about? Ken Blanchard, famous for his work developing the Situational Leadership model, offers this advice: Diagnose the situation first. Ask: "What is the task at hand, and what is this person's level of competency and commitment on this particular task?" ("Commitment," in this model, means a combination of motivation and confidence.) Once the factors for each situation are measured and assessed, the application of the appropriate balance of supportive and directive behaviors is imperative. Simple. (Not always easy, but simple.)

Here are a couple of examples:

- A high-performer, highly skilled, and confident at this assignment will require trust, support, and less instruction.
- A newbie, excited but raw, will need direction and boundaries, so they don't break things.

As you are well aware, everything is task-dependent; your employees may perform like Mick Jagger on one task and then tank like the dude at karaoke singing "Freebird" on another. No offense. To that guy or Lynyrd Skynyrd.

Or Mick Jagger.

Because he's Mick friggin' Jagger.

As the Rolling Stones have done for over a half-century and freestyle rappers do every night, you learn to improvise and adapt.

Using the principles laid out in *Acoustic Leadership* helps you improvise and adapt to something greater.

▶ Playlist

Title	Artist	Time
Dear Lord	John Coltrane; written by J. Coltrane (Verve, 1965).	5:31
Freebird	Lynyrd Skynyrd; written by A Collins, R. Van Zandt (Verve, 1973).	9:07
Beast of Burden	Rolling Stones; written by M. Jagger, K. Richards (Rolling Stones Records, 1978).	4:25

Visit ricklozano.com/resources for the complete Acoustic Leadership playlist.

III. The Wrap-Up

Now Kenny he's been mixing sound all evening
Sometimes I think that boy ain't got no ears
And Kathy's laughing
Kathy's always laughing
Well, keep on laughing Kathy
Just make it out of here.
It's closing time, unplug them people
And send them home
It's closing time

—L. Lovett

Closing Time

And the car's gonna roll where the wheels are pointed
And the day's gonna end where you are
And tomorrow
The world opens up again.

—R. Lozano

What's left when you let go?

Possibility.

A few years back, I wrote the lyrics to the song above, "What's Left When You Let Go." I was having a much-needed conversation with myself. "Stop getting in your own way, Rick. Let go of the fear. Embrace the passion. Step into the space you were meant to fill, and possibility will present itself." It was liberating to let go. Just as I felt when laying down the words to that song, I am grateful for the opportunity to share this work with you, and for what I have learned along the way.

So, there it is: Five hundred sixty-one million and one. (It is far more than that now, the number has grown to over a billion since I last looked.) We are nearing the end of our journey together, and I hope it has been a pleasant one! But just as I was sending this off for final publication, I came across one more testament to the power of Acoustic Leadership that I would be remiss if I did not share. And, just as the stars happen to align the way they do, it includes a term related to the world of music.

Be the buffer.

And adjust accordingly.

Modern recording technology is powerful, considerably upgraded and advanced since the days of Sir George Martin and The Beatles. Even on contemporary hardware, though, producing beautiful music is a mix of talent and resources balanced appropriately. The computer used to record music and the digital audio workstation (or DAW, the recording software we mentioned earlier) work effectively together in the studio only if something known as the "buffer" is set correctly.

In essence, buffer size determines how fast the computer processor can handle all the incoming and outgoing information that a DAW is generating and requires adjustment depending on what data it is presented with and what the recording engineer is trying to accomplish. Smaller buffer size equates to faster CPU processing and strains the system resources to their limit; larger buffer size is less strenuous on the CPU, but the information is processed more slowly and could crash the system if overtaxed.

The "right" buffer value is a compromise, a reorientation that best fits the situation and system requirements, and the setting has to be factored into the process so that every part of the system delivers its best output.

Could there be a more apt metaphor for leadership?

This, fittingly, brings us to Buffer, a company that specializes in social media tools.

Case Study

Buffer is an apropos illustration of the contemporary challenges many organizations increasingly face or will soon face. Buffer is global in nature, with employees in fifteen countries and physically dispersed; their eighty-five employees work remotely and have since 2015. They had long considered the potential benefits of moving to a 4-day workweek, and when the pandemic hit in 2020, they decided to do it, knowing the pressure that the COVID reality would place on employees, particularly parents working with children at home.

That was pretty much all I knew about Buffer, but as I learned more about them, I found that the principles laid out in Acoustic Leadership were on display everywhere in the company, including a forward-thinking leadership team at the helm. Here are a few examples with direct correlations to the pillars on which Acoustic Leadership is built, as well as some direct quotes from CEO and Co-Founder Joel Gascoigne, from a Twitter thread discussing their experiments:

Simplicity

Even before implementing 4-day workweeks, Buffer prioritized doing the right work instead of busywork and eschewed the traditional trappings and expectations of how and when work gets done. Asked if they would continue working with a 4-day schedule, CEO Gascoigne responded, "Ultimately, we will make our decision based on whether we achieve our goals as a company. I fundamentally believe though, that the 5-day workweek is a relic of the industrial era and not necessarily the most effective way to work." In another comment, he says, "The extra day builds in reflection time that we often don't make room for, where many of us solve problems. So, in many ways, we do more meaningful work."

Authenticity

Aligning people around "the why" is critical. Buffer reemphasized the team's vision and purpose, collective goals, and accountability to their work and – in keeping with one of their core values - transparently faced issues as they arose.

One could imagine, given the shorter timeframe and pressing business needs in the tech space, there would be the temptation to track people's actions. Instead, Buffer relies on trust. Says Gascoigne, "I think what really makes 4DWW effective is a culture of trust and a strong sense of purpose and shared values. Not tracking exact hours, and more focus on tracking output."

And they role model what they espouse. I assumed at first that the CEO and Founder would likely make space for everyone else to work fewer days but dutifully (and perhaps hypocritically) work when no one else was. It turns out he and the entire senior leadership team apply the same logic to their schedule. They are consistent in words and action.

Their say:do is not askew.

Opportunity

Previously, we highlighted the benefits Boston Consulting Group enjoyed as a result of their PTO program. As a refresher, participants took time off during their workweek to disconnect and rejuvenate and found themselves being more productive as they got better at prioritizing, delegating, and relying on each other to get work done.

Buffer also understands the business opportunity in unplugging; magic happens when we allow ourselves space and time to be mindful and unassaulted by constant inputs. Gascoigne describes, "The thing is, when you're working, you're not generally digesting and ruminating and having realizations."

Recent revelations in brain science reinforce this idea. Creativity and abstract connections are more likely to bloom during the times when our brains are "idle," engaged enough to be awake, but with the freedom to wander. Why do you think your best ideas come when you are walking or in the shower?

Gascoigne explains, "Most of the time, I've taken a complete break, which interestingly enough has turned out to be the thing that benefits the business the most. For me, the additional day helps me have more things rise from the subconscious to become epiphanies. I gain more clarity, which I can shift to better action."

Unplugged. More with less.

Muck be damned.

This is just one example of one leader at one company experimenting with new ways of working and adapting to change, and there is inherent risk singling out any one organization as the future holds secrets that we are not yet privy to. Today's tower of triumph could be tomorrow's tale of tragedy. But who cares?

Buffer is inspiring for just being willing to try and possibly fail.

At the end of the Twitter thread, which I'll make available in the reference section at the end of the book, the CEO ends by saying, "Last comment. And with all of that, I'd like to say: Try those wild ideas. Question the status quo and try improved approaches. Test whether those new ideas work, and adapt when they don't. But fight for a new idea, that still improves the status quo. The world needs that innovation."

Yes, it does.

You can help.

From muck to magic.

Start by taking immediate action.

I hope *Acoustic Leadership* has served its purpose as a guide to reimagine, reset, and build from these three essential areas: simplicity, authenticity, and opportunity. The pages of this book offer ideas, statistics, examples, and — hopefully — inspiration. To alleviate muck, create work cultures that matter, and unlock everyone's potential and talent in your organization.

And that, like the work of Penn and Teller, requires focus and execution. It depends upon action and results in magic.

Throughout this text, you have read ideas and suggestions for what is next. But, as with any book you read or training program you attend, what matters most is what you do with it. I encourage you to discuss, explore, and apply promptly. I recommend transparently introducing these concepts to your teams, initiate some of the dialogues found within, ask good questions and create a shared language and vision of what is possible.

Feel free to fail along the way.

And listen to some of the music referenced in the book while you are doing it. (And, yes, my original music is available on all the streaming services. I'm horrible about promoting it, but I am especially proud of the work I've done on my last two albums, and you might enjoy it. And — share some of your beloved tunes with me. I'm always on the hunt for my next favorite song!) And, since I am a student and learner myself, I always appreciate the sharing of ideas, successes, and challenges, so please feel free to share yours with me as well. I learn because others contribute, and I'll take what I learn and make it available to others.

For ideas, playlists, tools, inspiration, and resources from this book to take this journey forward, visit ricklozano.com/resources.

And that's it. That's Acoustic Leadership.

But every great show deserves an encore, so in that spirit, I leave you with...

The PFM.

The story of where it all began.

Before we adjourn, I would like to bring this exploration full circle (a *da capo al fine*, so to speak,) and to do so, I'm going to share with you the journey that led us to *Acoustic Leadership*. This story includes me, but it isn't about me. I tell it to give credit where credit is due and to illustrate how the simplicity, authenticity, and opportunity concepts helped us get here even if I didn't call them that or understand them in that form at the time.

I share this story to remind you of the influence you have on others.

A leader changed the course of my career, and I dare say, my life.

A statement like this doesn't always have a positive connotation but in this case, it does. And Larry Guillory is to blame.

LG, as he's sometimes called, was my manager for a while, and he entered my work world during a challenging time. My daily life was a little up in the air; work was a bit chaotic. Part of that chaos was because LG wasn't even my manager. He was my "grand boss," if you will. My previous manager had been fired and I skip-level reported to Larry.

I wasn't sure which end was up.

I didn't get a lot of face time with him as he was tied up in meetings most of the time (Hey, LG, reread the chapter on muck!), and each time I did meet with him, it seemed like the company had changed strategy and the requirements of my role.

It was frustrating. Every other week, the incessant changes would render the work I had just done irrelevant. I hesitated to start anything new, as I expected it would change by our next one-on-one.

(You've probably been there…frustrating, right?)

So, I was not surprised when yet another of the dreaded meetings didn't start very promisingly.

"All right, Rick. Man, I am so glad we get some time to chat today; I've meant to spend more time with you; sorry it has been crazy. This place is crazy!"

I should note he was still relatively new to the company at that point. And the place *was* crazy. A great place to work, but insane at times.

"I hear you. I'm feeling it too."

"What's on your mind, Rick? What do you want to talk about today?"

"Direction? Where are we going and what should I be doing because I'm a little lost right now."

"Yeah, I feel you. You know…okay…you know what? We'll get to that in a minute. Before we do, let's talk about you. What does Rick Lozano love?"

"Huh?"

"What do you love?"

(Pause.)

"Well, I would…love…some clarity around…."

"Yeah, we'll get to that. You, Rick. What does Rick Lozano love to do?"

I was getting a little irritated.

"I love facilitating and presenting to audiences where…."

"Yeah. Sure, but what does Rick *looove* to do?" He elongated the vowel sound as if that changed the nature of the question.

I responded, "Well, I *looove*…."

(Okay, I was totally irritated.)

"…the executive speaker development program we've rolled out, I …."

"Nah, no, man."

He waved his hand up in a gesture that indicated I wasn't understanding. He stood up, walked around, and rephrased the question.

"What does Rick love to do? I mean something that you crave."

"Where do you go when you lose track of time? Where everything just makes sense, and you could do it all day because you are just in the flow, and it is something you love to do?"

I looked up at him (he is quite tall) and asked, "At work?"

"Wherever. Whatever."

"Um…I'm a musician. I'm a singer. I'm a songwriter. I play guitar, harmonica, piano, some other stuff."

He asked slowly, "*Why* do you play music?"

I remember how poignant that question seemed in the moment. Why, indeed? Why do I play music? Why do I still write songs most people will never hear, why do I invest so much time and energy into a hobby that has never been a profit-based endeavor? Something about Larry's question made me think. Then smile.

"You know…I don't know. I've never really thought of it. It is just something I've done since I was a kid. Just who I am. I never really learned formally, I kind of taught myself. But you know what? Do you know what I love about music? Honestly, it is the one place I can go where I can do anything. There are no rules: I can create anything; I can say anything. I don't always know how or what I'm going to do, and I don't always have the technical ability but, still, music is the one place in life where I not only have an infinite capacity to create but complete ownership. Music is mine."

I was animated at this point.

Now LG was equally engaged. "That's it, man. Do more of that!"

"Yeah, well, I have a gig at this bar called Big Hops in a few…"

"No, man, do more of that *here!*"

(Pause.)

"...Here?"

"Yeah, here! I'm telling you, that's the Rick Lozano thing!"

"What's the Rick Lozano thing?"

"Music, man, do more of that here!"

"Um...what does that...*look like*?"

"Music, bring your guitar to work!"

"What does...*that*...look like?"

He stood up to leave.

"I don't know, man, but I'm telling you that's the Rick Lozano thing! Do more of that here!"

"How...do I make that *good*?"

"I don't know, man, but I'm telling you that's the Rick Lozano thing, do more of that here. Hey, this has been great, I gotta run, but we'll catch up soon. PFM man, just remember, PFM."

"What's PFM?"

"Pure friggin' magic man. Pure friggin' magic! That's how it's all gonna work, PFM."

And he left.

Larry Guillory's an idiot, I remember thinking. Pure friggin' magic? I didn't even get what I friggin' needed from this meeting! (For the record, he didn't say "friggin" and neither did I.)

What was I supposed to do with *that*? Pure friggin' magic. Larry's friggin' crazy!

What was I supposed to do, bring my guitar to work? We're doing compliance training!

And then a funny thing happened. I know this sounds hokey, but at that same time in my life, I had just come back from my first Association for Talent Development (ATD...formerly ASTD) International Conference, and I had attended a session on using improv techniques in team development. The principle idea being the "Yes, and..." concept. When someone offers you an idea, take it. Don't say no; move it forward.

I had my instructions. Make music here, in my role.

But how to make that work?

Take the idea, say yes, move it forward.

I had an upcoming team-building session. Maybe I could…. No. I shouldn't.
Wait — yes, and…

…click!

▌ Pure friggin' magic.

I brought my guitar to work. We used it in a team-building session I was running to write a song about their team. Then I brought my ukulele to our emerging leader cohort, and we wrote a song with the leaders there. My colleague, Ron Soos, one of the most talented presenters I know, came up with an idea for a talk show for our "rookie orientation" program — he was the host, and I was the musical sidekick.

And everything just clicked.

Music…work…training…songs…I found a sudden surge of energy, an increase in output, something was different. I wasn't always bringing my guitar to work, but I was thinking like a musician — at work.

And everything just clicked.

I decided to apply to speak at the ATD International Conference the following year, quite the long shot, seeing as how I wasn't really sure what I had to offer, wasn't a well-known "thought leader" (I hate that term) or anything like that. And given they get a thousand submissions every year and only a couple hundred are accepted, I figured, *Not a chance!*

It was that feeling of impossibility that helped me create my proposal. I wasn't going to get accepted; I might as well have fun with it, right? I came up with an idea; it sounded like a winner. I titled it "Sweet Caroline: A Super Setlist for Sensational Learning Sessions!" The description read:

What do the most effective facilitators and your favorite musicians have in common? Engaged audiences! In this session, we'll borrow some ideas from the world of music to help you create engagement in your learning programs. Rick Lozano, and his guitar, will introduce....

And I submitted it.

Hey, at least it was fun.

Work and life moved on, I got a new manager, still ran into LG here and there, and then months later, I got the email...

"ATD has accepted your proposal to speak at..."

What?

"Um...what the hell do I do now?"

I mean, I hadn't thought this the entire way through. I only created a concept; I didn't expect it to work! And I certainly didn't have any content!

I told LG. He was more excited than I was.

"What do you need, Rick? How can I support you?"

"Um...I don't know. I guess I need to build the session first, maybe?"

"Oh, that's easy, just keep doing what you are doing, PFM, I told you! Here's what I'll do to support you...."

And support he did. To start, a budget of two thousand dollars. On top of paying for travel and expenses! *Unheard of!* Money? For a session that I hadn't even created? What was I even supposed to spend it on?

He also gave me support in the form of graphic design help. He had me meet with Ernest Flores, a talented designer who took my idea and created a very cool logo as well as some PowerPoint templates. Working with Ernest inspired me. His enthusiasm for my concept blew me away, and his creative talent made me realize that I had to make my session at least as captivating as his design! I owed him that much.

He came up with an idea to create small notebooks that looked like the front and back of cover art for a vinyl album. It had a nifty design on the front, a hole in the lid where an amplifier poked through from the second page, simulating a vinyl record sticking out through the packaging. It had a tracklist on the back, just like an album. We printed five hundred of them. It rocked.

And everything changed.

I had no idea it would work out, but there was some buzz around my concept. The ballroom filled to max capacity 30 minutes before the session began. Standing room only. In true rock-and-roll fashion, cops arrived before I even started speaking! We had way too many people in the room, and we were not in compliance with the fire code. So they kicked people out.

(And even more rock-and-roll, quite a few of them waited for the po-po to leave then snuck back in!)

I was nervous but ecstatic. I incorporated my guitar at several points in the session, presented my butt off, tried my best just to do what I do best. PFM, right?

I got a standing ovation.

From there, my career took a different turn. This evolved identity coalesced the perfect combination of my experience, expertise, and talents. I started thinking like a musician and a songwriter at work, believing in myself, and forcing myself to work harder than ever, energized by this mysterious-yet-powerful momentum. An opportunity had appeared that I could never have imagined, at least not on my own.

Larry's PFM *changed the way I think.*

And you now hold the strange culmination of all those efforts in the form of *Acoustic Leadership. Develop a Leadership Culture That Resonates.*

Thanks, LG.

As I deconstruct all the paths of this crazy journey, I am still astonished at how it all came together, how one action led to another, and how it somehow made sense. LG's encouragement to "do more of that here" was the catalyst. As a leader, he profoundly influenced me.

And now, maybe you, too. Some PFM, leadership support, trust, and advocacy ignited my imagination and drove me to craft my Acoustic

Leadership teachings, and this work wouldn't exist if not for him. It's also important to note that he is not some magical deity, some guru who holds all the answers and is only accessible at high & remote elevations. He is another fellow imperfect human. He didn't know what he was doing when he inspired me with PFM, but his instinctive approach naturally maps to the three foundations:

- *Simplicity*: Go for it. With blind faith and a little PFM, he gave me the permission and resources (including money!) to roll with a crazy idea I hadn't even built yet. No muck, no fuss — go for it! I believe in you.
- *Authenticity*: Trust. Safety. It's okay if it isn't perfect; even if it fails, this is a new chance to do something different. Own it. Be yourself.
- *Opportunity*: My strengths, my jet stream, paired with talented partners that forced me to up my game, produced a profound change in how I thought about my work. And myself.

A leader helped unlock the next stage of my career using these three Acoustic Leadership concepts.

Now it is your turn to resonate.

Create PFM.

And the beat goes on...

I leave you with the rhythm rolling around in my brain...

We've explored the world from Austin to Japan. Bucked the muck and joined a band. Navigated through noise, found clarity in the clouds. Influence, impact, motivate crowds. Authenticity clues, performance reviews, and more effective meetings. Greenhouses that tend the soil, growing oaks from tiny seedlings. The Beatles, "Freebird", "Osaka in the Rain". Jagger, Buffett, Ella, Coltrane. You've heard the stats, my Australian cats, read the stories, seized the glory. Open your eyes with nary a blink, this is your time, your chance to rethink. To build, innovate. Lead, resonate. Develop, elevate. Inspire, reverberate. Unplugged. Acoustic. Triumph from tragic. And now it's time for...

Pure friggin' magic.

Thank you for the work you do.

I hope this finds you laughing.

(And maybe singing. Or at least humming along.)

—Rick

▶ Playlist

Title	Artist	Time
Closing Time	Lyle Lovett; written by L. Lovett (MCA, 1986).	3:44
What's Left When You Let Go	Rick Lozano; written by R. Lozano (Lozano, 2020).	3:29
Sweet Caroline	Neil Diamond; written by N. Diamond (Universal Music, 1972).	3:24
The Beat Goes On (The Sonny and Cher Song)	Sonny & Cher; written by S. Bono (Atco, 1967).	3:18

Visit ricklozano.com/resources for the complete Acoustic Leadership playlist.

References

Chapter 1

Aaron Schwartz, "The Science of Talent Attraction: Understanding What Makes People Click," Indeed.com, September 2, 2020, http://offers.indeed.com/rs/699-SXJ-715/images/Deerfield_Beach_Explore_Q415.pdf.

Jim Harter, "Employee Engagement on the Rise in the U.S.," Gallup, August 26, 2018, https://news.gallup.com/poll/241649/employee-engagement-rise.aspx.

The Work Trend Index, "The Next Great Disruption Is Hybrid Work- Are We Ready?" Microsoft, March 2021, https://www.microsoft.com/en-us/worklab/work-trend-index.

Gary Hamel and Michele Zanini, "Excess Management Is Costing the US $3 Trillion Per Year," *Harvard Business Review*, September 5, 2016, https://hbr.org/2016/09/excess-management-is-costing-the-us-3-trillion-per-year.

Jim Harter, "Employee Engagement on the Rise in the US," Gallup, August 26, 2018, https://news.gallup.com/poll/241649/employee-engagement-rise.aspx.

Wikipedia, "Dunning-Kruger Effect," September 2, 2020, https://en.wikipedia.org/wiki/Dunning–Kruger_effect.

US Office of Personnel Management, "Leadership Competency Proficiency Levels," OPM.gov, July 23, 2020 https://www.opm.gov/policy-data-oversight/assessment-and-selection/competencies.

Chapter 3

Eric Ries, *The Lean Startup: How Today's Entrepreneurs Use Continuous Innovation to Create Radically Successful Business*, (Strawberry Hills, NSW, Australia: Currency, 2011).

Chee Tung Leong, "Tech Leaders Run Their Companies Differently, and Their Teams Are 40% More Productive as a Result," Forbes, August 15, 2017, https://www.forbes.com/sites/cheetung/2017/08/15/tech-leaders-run-their-companies-differently-and-their-teams-love-them-for-it/#6d798d21565e.

Gary Hamel and Michele Zanini, "What We Learned about Bureaucracy from 7,000 Harvard Business Review Readers," August 10, 2017, https://hbr.org/2017/08/what-we-learned-about-bureaucracy-from-7000-hbr-readers.

Chapter 4

Gary Hamel and Michele Zanini, "What We Learned about Bureaucracy from 7,000 HBR Readers," August 10, 2017, https://hbr.org/2017/08/what-we-learned-about-bureaucracy-from-7000-hbr-readers.

Oxford Languages, "Bureaucracy definition," Google.com, accessed September 2, 2020, https://www.google.com/search?q=bureacracy+definition.

Society for Human Resource Management, "SHRM/Globoforce Using Recognition and Other Workplace Efforts to Engage Employees," January 24, 2018, https://www.shrm.org/hr-today/trends-and-forecasting/research-and-surveys/pages/employee-recognition-2018; https://go.globoforce.com/rs/globoforce/images/SHRM_Spring2013_web.pdf.

SHRM.org, "Performance Management That Makes A Difference: An Evidence- Based Approach," December 17th, 2017, https://www.shrm.org/hr-today/trends-and-forecasting/special-reports-and-expert-views/documents/performance%20management.pdf.

Thomas H. Davenport, Jeanne Harris, and Jeremy Shapiro, "Competing on Talent Analytics," *Harvard Business Review*, October 2010, https://hbr.org/2010/10/competing-on-talent-analytics.

Gary Hamel and Michele Zanini, "The $3 Trillion Prize for Busting Bureaucracy (and How to Claim It)," GaryHamel.com, March 2016, http://www.garyhamel.com/sites/default/files/uploads/three-trillion-dollars.pdf.

Stephanie Vozza, "Why Employees at Apple and Google Are More Productive," March 13, 2017, https://www.fastcompany.com/3068771/how-employees-at-apple-and-google-are-more-productive.

II. THE SOLUTION

Chapter 5

Holacracy, "Why Practice Holacracy?" Holacracy.org, accessed April 12, 2020, https://www.holacracy.org/explore/why-practice-holacracy.

Piotr Majchrzak, "Our Holacracy Experience: What It Is and Why It Works," Medium.com, March 5, 2018, https://medium.com/@piotrmajchrzak/our-holacracy-experience-what-it-is-and-why-it-works-564a36bdfbd7.

Zappos, "Holacracy and Self-Organization," ZapposInsights.com, accessed September 2, 2020, https://www.zapposinsights.com/about/holacracy.

Handelsbanken, "Our Story," Handelsbanken.com, accessed September 2, 2020, https://www.handelsbanken.com/en/about-the-group/our-story.

Warren Berger, *The Book of Beautiful Questions: The Powerful Questions That Will Help You Decide, Create, Connect, and Lead* (New York: Bloomsbury Publishing, 2018).

Reed Hastings, "Netflix Culture: Freedom and Responsibility," Slideshare, August 1, 2009, https://www.slideshare.net/reed2001/culture-1798664.

Netflix, "Netflix Culture," Netflix.com, accessed September 2, 2020, https://jobs.netflix.com/culture.

Steven M.R. Covey. *The Speed of Trust* (Salt Lake City: FranklinCovey, 2008).

Alexander Westerdahl, "Seven Months with Flexible Public Holidays," Spotify.com, June 29, 2018, https://hrblog.spotify.com/2018/06/29/seven-months-with-flexible-public-holidays.

Francesca Gino, "Rebel Talent," HBR.org, October-November 2016, https://www.hbs.edu/faculty/Publication%20Files/Let%20your%20workers%20rebel_b87d0da9-de68-45be-a026-22dee862e6e4.pdf

Ritz Carlton Leadership Center, "The Power of Empowerment," RitzCarltonLeadershipCenter.com, March 19, 2019, https://ritzcarltonleadershipcenter.com/2019/03/19/the-power-of-empowerment.

Stanford University, "How to Identify and Remove Five Common Causes of Organizational Drag," HRdive.com, October 25, 2016, https://www.hrdive.com/spons/how-to-identify-and-remove-5-common-causes-of-organizational-drag/428828.

Gary Hamel and Michele Zanini, "What We Learned about Bureaucracy from 7,000 HBR Readers," *Harvard Business Review*, August 10, 2017, https://hbr.org/2017/08/what-we-learned-about-bureaucracy-from-7000-hbr-readers.

Desmond Leach, Steven Rogelberg, Peter Warr, and Jennifer Burnfield, "Perceived Meeting Effectiveness: The Role of Design Characteristics," *Journal of Business and Psychology*, 24 (March 2009), 65–76, https://www.researchgate.net/publication/227024372_Perceived_Meeting_Effectiveness.

Cal Newport, *Deep Work: Rules for Focused Success in a Distracted World* (New York: Grand Central Publishing, 2016).

Desmond Leach, Steven Rogelberg, Peter Warr, and Jennifer Burnfield, "Perceived Meeting Effectiveness: The Role of Design Characteristics," *Journal of Business and Psychology*, 24 (March 2009), 65–76, https://www.researchgate.net/publication/227024372_Perceived_Meeting_Effectiveness.

Patrick Lencioni, *The Five Dysfunctions of a Team: A Leadership Fable* (San Francisco: Jossey-Bass, 2002).

The Work Trend Index, "The Next Great Disruption Is Hybrid Work- Are We Ready?" Microsoft, March 2021, https://www.microsoft.com/en-us/worklab/work-trend-index.

Bill Chappell, "Four-Day Workweek Boosted Workers' Productivity by 40 Percent, Microsoft Japan Says," NPR.org, November 4, 2019, https://www.npr.org/2019/11/04/776163853/microsoft-japan-says-4-day-workweek-boosted-workers-productivity-by-40.

David Graeber, *Bullshit Jobs: A Theory*, (New York City: Simon & Schuster, 2018).

Charles Rogel, "How Much Do Performance Reviews Really Cost and Are They Really Worth It?" Decisionwise.com, accessed September 2, 2020, https://decision-wise.com/how-much-do-performance-reviews-actually-cost-and-are-they-really-worth-it.

Robert Sutton and Ben Wigert, "More Harm Than Good: The Truth about Performance Reviews," Gallup, May 6, 2019, https://www.gallup.com/workplace/249332/harm-good-truth-performance-reviews.aspx.

Peter Cappelli and Anna Tavis, "The Performance Management Revolution," *Harvard Business Review*, October 2016, https://hbr.org/2016/10/the-performance-management-revolution.

Nitin Nohria and Michael Beer, "Cracking the Code of Change," *Harvard Business Review*, May–June 2000, https://hbr.org/2000/05/cracking-the-code-of-change.

Johanna Bolin Tingvall, "Why Individual OKRs Don't Work for Us," Spotify.com, August 15, 2016, https://hrblog.spotify.com/2016/08/15/our-beliefs.

Michael Winnick, "Putting a Finger on Our Phone Obsession," DScout.com, June 16, 2016, https://blog.dscout.com/mobile-touches#1.

John Gall, *Systemantics: How Systems Really Work and Especially How They Fail* (New York City: Quadrangle, 1977).

Chapter 6

Alex Coletti, "Unplugged Interview" with Eric Clapton, *Guitar World*, June 1993, http://www.iem.ac.ru/clapton/articles/interview.unplugged.html.

John Maxwell, 2019 National Speakers Association annual conference.

Mary Hayes, Fran Chumney, Corrine Wright, and Marcus Buckingham, "The Global Study of Engagement: Technical Report," *ADP Research Institute*, September 2, 2020, https://www.adp.com/resources/articles-and-insights/articles/g/global-study-of-engagement-technical-report.aspx.

Leslie Perlow, Constance Noonan Hadley, and Eunice Eun, "Stop the Meeting Madness," *Harvard Business Review*, July–August 2017, https://hbr.org/2017/07/stop-the-meeting-madness.

Desmond Leach, Steven Rogelberg, Peter Warr, Jennifer Burnfield, "Perceived Meeting Effectiveness: The Role of Design Characteristics," *Journal of Business and Psychology*, 24 (March 2009), 65–76, https://www.researchgate.net/publication/227024372_Perceived_Meeting_Effectiveness.

Murielle Tiambo, "Leaders Can Cultivate True Employee Empowerment," *Forbes*, February 19, 2019, https://www.forbes.com/sites/strategyand/2019/02/19/leaders-can-cultivate-true-employee-empowerment/#ce059353ab19.

Robert Sutton, *The No Asshole Rule: Building a Civilized Workplace and Surviving One That Isn't* (New York: Business Plus, September 1, 2010).

Julia Rozovsky, "The Five Keys to a Successful Google Team," reWork, November 17, 2015, https://rework.withgoogle.com/blog/five-keys-to-a-successful-google-team.

Frances J. Milliken, Elizabeth W. Morrison, and Patricia F. Hewlin, "An Exploratory Study of Employee Silence: Issues that Employees Don't Communicate Upward and Why," New York University Stern School of Business, November 4, 2003, http://homepages.se.edu/cvonbergen/files/2012/12/AN-EXPLORATORY-STUDY-OF-EMPLOYEE-SILENCE_IISSUES-THAT-EMPLOYEES-DONT-COMMUNICATE-UPWARD-AND-WHY.pdf.

Gino Wickman, *Traction: Get a Grip on Your Business* (Benbella: Dallas, 2011).

"ADP Research Institute Sets International Benchmark for Employee Engagement with its 19-Country Global Study of Engagement," June 6, 2019, https://mediacenter.adp.com/2019-06-14-ADP-Research-Institute-Sets-International-Benchmark-for-Employee-Engagement-with-its-19-Country-Global-Study-of-Engagement.

Tiny Pulse, "Seven Vital Trends Disrupting Today's Workforce: Results and Data from 2013 TinyPulse Employee Engagement Survey," TinyPulse.com, 2013, https://www.tinypulse.com/resources/employee-engagement-survey-2013.

Britt Andreatta, *Wired to Connect: The Brain Science of Teams and A New Model for Creating Collaboration and Inclusion* (7th Mind Publishing: Santa Barbara, 2018).

Spotify, "The Band Manifesto," SpotifyJobs.com, accessed September 2, 2020, https://www.spotifyjobs.com/the-band-manifesto.

Daniel M. Cable, Francesca Gino, and Bradley R. Staats, "Breaking Them in or Eliciting Their Best? Reframing Socialization around Newcomers' Authentic Self-Expression," *Administrative Science Quarterly*, 58 (March 2013), https://repository.upenn.edu/mgmt_papers/82.

Sensoree, "Mood sweaters," accessed September 30, 2020, http://moodsweater.com.

Chapter 7

Beverly Kaye and Julie Winkle Giulioni, *Help Them Grow or Watch Them Go: Career Conversations Organizations Need and Employees Want* (Oakland: Berrett-Koehler Publishers, 2019).

Beverly Kaye and Sharon Jordan-Evans, *Love 'Em or Lose 'Em: Getting Good People to Stay* (Oakland, CA: Berrett-Koehler Publishers, 2014).

Jeff Highly, "Build a career path for your technical individual contributors — here's how," Rackspace Technology Blog, August 4th, 2020, https://www.rackspace.com/blog/build-career-path-technical-individual-contributors.

Michael Bungay Stanier, *The Coaching Habit: Say Less, Ask More, and Change the Way You Lead Forever* (Vancouver, BC: Page Two Books, 2016).

Liz Wiseman and Greg McKeown, *Multipliers: How the Best Leaders Make Everyone Smarter* (New York: Harper Collins, 2010).

Eleanor Ainge Roy, "No Downside: New Zealand Firm Adopts Four-Day Week after Successful Trial, TheGuardian.com, October, 2018, https://www.theguardian.com/world/2018/oct/02/no-downside-new-zealand-firm-adopts-four-day-week-after-successful-trial.

Rick Jernigan and Kelley Freeman, *C.O.A.C.H The Final Act of Leading is Leaving* (Dallas: Align Group Press, 2010).

III. THE WRAP UP

Chapter 8

Kory Grow, "John Coltrane Wants to Be 'Force for Good' in Rare Interview," Rolling Stone.com, May 12, 2015, https://www.rollingstone.com/music/music-news/john-coltrane-wants-to-be-force-for-good-in-rare-interview-178182.

Dictionary.com, "Resonance," accessed September 2, 2020, https://www.dictionary.com/browse/resonance?s=t.

Julian Birkinshaw and Jordan Cohen, "Make Time for the Work That Matters," *Harvard Business Review*, September 2013, https://hbr.org/2013/09/make-time-for-the-work-that-matters.

John Medina, *Brain Rules: 12 Principles for Surviving and Thriving at Work, Home, and School* (Seattle: Pear Press, 2008).

Michael Hines, "Goldman Sachs Is Giving Its Most Entrepreneurial Employees a Paid Two-Year Break to Launch Startups," Builtin.com, November 14, 2019, https://builtin.com/corporate-innovation/goldman-sachs-accelerate.

Leigh Buchanan, "Welcome to the Church of Fail," Inc.com, November 2019, https://www.inc.com/magazine/201311/leigh-buchanan/nixonmcinnes-innovation-by-celebrating-mistakes.html.

Joanna Barsh, Marla M. Capozzi, and Jonathan Davidson, "Leadership and Innovation," McKinsey Quarterly, January 1, 2008, https://www.mckinsey.com/business-functions/strategy-and-corporate-finance/our-insights/leadership-and-innovation.

Paul Hersey, Kenneth Blanchard, and Dewey Johnson, *Management of Organizational Behavior* (New York: Pearson, 2012).

Joel Gasgoigne, Buffer. Twitter thread, January 2021. https://twitter.com/joelgascoigne/status/1340124194000912390.

Liner Notes

Thanks to Jenefer Angell, who took my original, chaotic work and helped me focus it and create something great. Her editing unlocked the potential in this book and her work at PassionfruitProjects.com is phenomenal.

Regina Pfohl, thanks for helping finalize the final feel and flow.

Erica Russell, your designs have been the backbone for this journey as it has evolved, I couldn't have done it without you!

Thanks to Tim Slade for making the final product look awesome. You rock, Tim.

To Jonathan Magid, your support and unwavering belief in me helped me believe this was possible.

Hey, LG…thanks for the PFM! Look at what you started!

Linda Swindling, Merit Kahn, Roger Wolkoff, Amy McWhirter, Laura Bonich, thanks for sharing your insight, passion, and awesomeness!

My SFU brain trust and all my colleagues, you have been the biggest part of my growth in the last year. Thank you from the bottom of my heart!

My NSA family, I have learned so much from you and am continually inspired by you.

Big thanks to Brian Walter who took the time to help a stranger find his "rickness."

To the leaders I've been fortunate enough to work with and learn from, you inspired this and made me want to do better.

Theresa Hoehne, I could have used you as an example in every section.

To the emerging leader cohorts through the years – who was coaching who exactly? ;)

To my friends at ATD headquarters: Justin, Apryl, Teona, Steve, Alexandria and the entire crew, your friendship, advocacy, and support have been a constant source of positivity and learning in my career. Special shout out to Bridget Dunn, you da bomb.com.

To my entire ATD/L&D community and all those I've learned from, spent time with, shared a meal or a beer with, celebrated with at networking night, and those of you who show up every year and inspire me to keep doing what I'm doing, it matters more than you can imagine and I'm grateful! The best learning of my career was time spent with and around you. Dan Steer, Britt Andreatta, Becca Clanton, Meghan Styles, Ismael Allawala, James Haak, Stacey Gordon, Kate Pinto, Dawn Mahoney, Doug DeLuca, Doug Smith, Paul Boeffler, Julie Dirksen, Clark Quinn, Trista Taylor, Becca Wilson, JD Dillon, Travis Waugh, Bianca Woods, way more of you than I can fit in this section, but you know who you are and are a big part of the gratitude I feel.

To my ATD TechKnowledge PAC peeps, so glad our paths crossed, I've learned something from every one of you.

To my Racker family, all of you. Thank you isn't enough. Thanks for letting me share your user guide, Cat!

To Ernest, your enthusiasm and creativity helped unlock mine. Thanks to you and J-Hopps for being there when it all exploded!

To the musicians in my life who I've had the great fortune of sharing a stage, front porch, or campfire with. Your creative energy found its way into this book. Doug Schmude, Andrew Dunbar, Roger Winn, Duane Allee, the guys in CrossCurrent who taught me how to rock, the miscreants at Joe's Bar, the crew at Black Mountain College and Troupe Texas, I'll never forget.

To the musicians mentioned in this book, and the millions that aren't, thanks for sharing your talents and passion with the world.

To Mom and Dad, your example of serving others with compassion inspires me to serve further.

To Dave, thanks for the help with the early edits and always inspiring me to be better.

To T-Bone, Linda, Ryan, Evan and the rest of la familia — I love you crazy fools.

Thanks to Jelly Dos and Loukie, two crazy kitties who chewed on my power cords as I wrote this book and continually made me smile.

And, of course, to Angela. My wife/manager/roadie/advisor/
consultant/executive chef/editor/head/lover/parole officer/scuba buddy/
partner in crime and love of my life. You are the most beautiful, thoughtful,
and loving person I know. You make me laugh like no one can and inspire
me to think of words and put them in songs.

The World Is an Ocean

And we are just the waves.

The world is an ocean. And we are just the waves.

A Chicago-area musician by the name of Michael Heaton wrote these lines. The recording of the song is minimalistic, just acoustic guitars and Michael's voice, it's a sparse production but it needs nothing more. Simple, thoughtful, beautiful.

I virtually met Michael almost 20 years ago in an online forum for independent musicians called Garageband.com. The platform was a place for independent musicians to host their music and gain exposure, but another big motivation to use the site was an opportunity to win a recording contract, every independent musician's dream at the time.

Paying $19.99 gave you entry into the contest or you could qualify by reviewing other people's songs in exchange. I was broke, so I listened to and reviewed quite a few songs. "Wildflower," a song Michael had written and performed, showed up in my review list. It was outstanding. Far better than most of the amateur uploads people like me had submitted, it was exceptionally well-produced, and the song itself just spoke to me. I loved it.

I didn't know it, but I needed that song in my life at that moment. Things were a mess. If you were to listen to the songs that I uploaded to Garageband.Com at that same time, you'd hear the voice, lyrics, and music of someone who was sad, angry, and confused. The songs were a reflection of the reality I was surrounded by, the tragic circumstances surrounding my first marriage (that's another book), and something about the bittersweet images in Wildflower moved me.

I reviewed the song favorably, of course, and also included some ideas of what the imagery in the song meant to me…loss, hope, beauty amid sadness. I mentioned in my review that this song made me happy at a point in my life when I could use it.

And I guess that moved Michael. He emailed me shortly afterward, which wasn't common at that time or on that platform, thanked me for the review, and told me the circumstances under which he wrote that song. His young niece (or nephew…I might be misremembering) had died unexpectedly.

I guess tragedy connects people.

We started up a discussion about music and stayed in contact for a little while. Michael encouraged me to keep doing what I was doing regardless of what the world said, that it would all come to mean something at some point. I appreciated that. He was much further along as a musician than I was, and I was grateful. I became a big fan of his. I always meant to find a way to get up to the Chicago area to see him play live, but I never did. I just listened to his albums as they came out.

Not too long ago, I was wondering why I hadn't seen any new music from him in a while, so I Googled to find out. It turns out he was preoccupied.

Cancer.

Damnit.

I contributed to the GoFundMe account created to help offset the family's medical costs — what else can you do? I thought about reaching out, but he wouldn't remember who I was, no point. I posted a get-well message on the board, then listened to his first album, *Learning Curve*, in its entirety.

Hold on to your memories/Cause they're the only things that you can save/The world is an ocean/And we are just the waves.

Michael died while I was writing this book. He was 53.

I was in my home office, working on the first draft of this book. I took a break and checked my email. The sad news was sent to the people following his progress through the fund. I cried surprisingly hard for someone I never had the chance to meet.

The power of music. The language of us all. I'm grateful for it and the smiles and community music brings.

Thank you, Michael. For your music and your words.

They gave me comfort as I found myself in tears again, mourning the loss of my nephew, Robert "Oso" Cruz, who we lost last year at the age of 22, also from cancer.

Also a musician.

The world is an ocean. And we are just the waves.

And, for the record, it did come to mean something. It always meant something. Some might say it was pure friggin' magic.

In loving memory of Robert "Oso" Cruz. We love you, Osoman.

▶ Playlist

Title	Artist	Time
Wildflower	Michael Heaton; written by M. Heaton (Alcachofra, 2003).	3:36
The World Is An Ocean	Michael Heaton; written by M. Heaton (Alcachofra, 2000).	5:04

Visit ricklozano.com/resources for the complete Acoustic Leadership playlist.

Up Front - On the Microphone, Rhythm and Lead Guitar...

Rick Lozano, CSP, helps people unlock potential and amplify their talent, and he does it all with his unique blend of energy, expertise, and a musician's soul.

With 20 years of experience in award-winning talent and leadership-development programs, Rick gives organizations, teams, and leaders the tools they need to thrive. Whether he is facilitating workshops online or in person, onstage as a keynote speaker or performer, or chatting casually one-on-one, Rick brings his internationally-acclaimed insight, charisma, and authenticity to everything he does. His refreshing talks, workshops, and performances leave audiences raving and, more importantly, heading back to work with action items they can immediately implement to produce change.

Rick is the 2021 president-elect of the Austin chapter of the National Speakers Association and holds the Certified Speaking Professional (CSP) designation, a credential earned by only the top echelon of professional speakers through the National Speakers Association. He has served on the Program Advisory Committee for the ATD (Association for Talent Development) TechKnowledge conference for three years and has contributed content and ideas to numerous national publications.

Rick integrates his musical lens into the work that he does as a speaker, author, and consultant, and also continues to perform, record, and draw on music as both the source — and the output — of inspiration and creativity in all his endeavors. He has self-produced six albums of original music to date and was a finalist in a national community radio songwriting competition. You can listen to most of his music wherever you stream it.

He and his wife Angela spend their spare time indulging their passion for scuba diving, hiking, biking, and live in San Antonio with two kids, two cats, and too many guitars.

From Inspiration to Action

The pages in this book are just the starting point. To help further instill these concepts in your organization and create long-lasting transformation with your teams, reach out today to inquire about solutions in the form of workshops, coaching, consulting, and keynote presentations at RickL@ RickLozano.com. You can also visit RickLozano.com or just pick up the phone and dial 720-935-8033. Let's Unlock & Amplify® the talent and potential around you and within you.

Testimonials

In my 25+ years' experience working in corporate settings, I can honestly say that Rick is one of the top coaches and facilitators I have had the pleasure of working with. He is highly knowledgeable about learning and development as a discipline as well as an amazing speaker.

—Debbie Talley, Rackspace Hosting

I attended your speaking engagement yesterday with UHS and let me tell you, it was amazing!! I loved it. As a fellow music lover, I can't recall the last time someone caught my attention and was able to keep it! What you do is pretty spectacular and thank you for sharing your gift with us. I am hoping to follow through with some of the amazing concepts you mentioned, I really hope to catch more of your speaking engagements in the near future.

—C.L., Project Coordinator, University Health System

I have had the privilege of planning our conferences for the last 10 years. It is a conference planner's dream to have your participants fully engaged, joining heartily in singing along, and ending with a rousing and well-deserved standing ovation. He was very thorough in assuring advance understanding or the needs of our participants and effective in translating those into a powerful program. Rock on!!!

—Wayne Drummond, Georgia Professional Human Services Association

We hired Rick Lozano for our keynote speaker at our annual Client Summit. Our Client Summit is the biggest event that we put on every year, so finding the right person for our final presentation is extremely important. Rick came highly recommended from one of our employees who saw him present at another conference and we immediately connected with Rick. Rick was very professional and always came prepared to our meetings, recommended content to us, and was very engaged the months leading up to the event. I was totally impressed that Rick catered his presentation to our company values, clients, and mission. It wasn't anything we had discussed but it truly showed Rick's aptitude to go above and beyond! I was blown away by his energy, ability to get the audience involved, and message during the presentation—and I know others were too! I would highly recommend Rick for any corporate Keynote presentation! Rick Lozano is INCREDIBLE!

—Olivia Sekarak, rev.io

Rick takes keynotes to the next level in both content and delivery. I recently attended Rick's keynote during a year that exposed the good, the bad, and the ugly of virtual speaking. His use of the virtual space was nothing short of innovative, and his ability to interweave content into his creative delivery resulted in a rich and impactful learning experience. Moreover, Rick knows how to have fun. I do not think I've ever smiled or laughed as much during a keynote as I did with his. The entire group left the session excited and energized.

—K.Z., Global Business Trainer, ATD San Antonio

WOW!!! I would take this course all day, every day! Rick was engaging, funny, and enlightening! His energy and knowledge was contagious! WOW!!!

—Participant, Leadership Development Training

Rick Lozano is world-class training guru, keynote speaker, musician, and wonderful person rolled into one. I can honestly say Rick has profoundly shaped my career since it was his class that got me started on the path to facilitation. I've had the privilege of being not only his student but partnering together on a few projects and can't speak highly enough of Rick's passion and talent for educating others. If you have the chance to take one of Rick's classes, hear him speak at a conference or catch one of his gigs, consider yourself among the fortunate!

—Liz Jurewicz, IBM

Rick Lozano recently spoke at the IEHRA Annual Conference for HR Professionals. His presentation was innovative, high energy and well received by our members. If your organization is looking for a presenter to discuss employee engagement, contact Rick for your next event.

—Karen Lombardi, IEHRA

Amazeballs! This session was so good I can't find a string of emojis that would do it justice. The best, most captivating session I have ever attended.

—Participant, ATD International Conference

Rick is an amazing and energetic speaker. His energy, passion, and profound lessons inspired and entertained our members as they take on the challenging task of employee engagement. Rick was energizing yet insightful and utilizing his great sense of humor brought a lot of fun to the session.

—Joan Maddux, Austin Contact Center Alliance

I only wish the session were longer! I could listen to him all day and I can't wait to get back to my space and find out what my people do that takes them to their happy place- and support them in doing more of that!

—Attendee, ATD International Conference

Made in the USA
Middletown, DE
06 January 2022